WHERE THERE IS LIGHT

PARAMAHANSA YOGANANDA

(1893–1952)

WHERE THERE IS LIGHT

Insight and Inspiration
for Meeting Life's Challenges

Selections from the teachings of
Paramahansa Yogananda

SELF-REALIZATION FELLOWSHIP
Founded by Paramahansa Yogananda

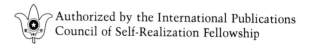 Authorized by the International Publications
Council of Self-Realization Fellowship

Self-Realization Fellowship was founded in 1920 by
Paramahansa Yogananda as the instrument for the
worldwide dissemination of his teachings. The reader
can be certain of the authenticity of writings and re-
cordings by or about Paramahansa Yogananda and his
teachings if the registered Self-Realization emblem,
and/or the statement of authorization (shown together above), appears on that work.

Library of Congress Catalog Number: 88–063330
ISBN 0-87612-275-6 (hardcover)
ISBN 0-87612-276-4 (paperback)
Printed in the United States of America

10854–65432

Contents

Publisher's Note

Since Paramahansa Yogananda's *Autobiography of a Yogi* was first published in 1946, his writings have received recognition in all parts of the world — from the literary and general public as well as from his followers. It is therefore not surprising that there are now a number of other publishers, organizations, and individuals claiming to represent his teachings. Readers sometimes inquire how they can be sure that a publication accurately presents Paramahansa Yogananda's life and teachings. In response to these inquiries, we would like to explain that Paramahansa Yogananda founded Self-Realization Fellowship in 1920 as the instrument for worldwide dissemination of his teachings. He personally chose and trained those close disciples who constitute the Self-Realization Fellowship Publications Council, giving them specific guidelines for the publishing of his writings, lectures, and *Self-Realization Lessons*. The presence in a publication of the emblem originated by Paramahansa Yogananda as the identifying symbol of his work and teachings (shown above) or the statement, "Authorized by the International Publications Council of Self-Realization Fellowship," assures the reader of the authenticity of that work.

SELF-REALIZATION FELLOWSHIP

Preface

BY SRI DAYA MATA

*President and spiritual head of Self-Realization
Fellowship/Yogoda Satsanga Society of India*

During the years in which I was blessed to receive
the spiritual training of Paramahansa Yogananda,* I came
to see that the mark of true wisdom is twofold: First, it
encompasses every aspect of our being—body, mind, and
soul; our personal lives as well as our relationships with
family, community, and the world. At the same time,
it is so simple and direct that we inwardly feel, "Yes, of
course! I have always known that!" There is a sense of
reawakening to an understanding that was already present within. When we are touched on this deeper level,
truth is instantly translated from mere philosophy into
active, workable solutions to our problems.

Such were the truths that flowed in a ceaseless
stream from my guru, Paramahansa Yogananda—not as
theological abstractions or platitudes, but as practical
expressions of that supreme wisdom which brings success, health, enduring happiness, and divine love into
all the circumstances of life. Though the full range and
depth of Paramahansaji's† teachings fills many volumes,
we are pleased to present in this compilation a few of
the individual gems of thought that sparkle throughout
his writings and lectures—profound truths conveyed in
a few potent words that kindle a renewed awareness of

* Sri Daya Mata entered the Self-Realization Fellowship monastic order in 1931, and received spiritual training directly from Paramahansa Yogananda for over twenty years. She was chosen by him to be
the third president and representative spiritual head of his worldwide
society, a position she has held from 1955 to the present.

† *Ji* is a suffix denoting respect.

our limitless inner resources, and that provide a reassuring sense of direction in times of uncertainty or crisis.

It was these innate capabilities of strength and intuitive understanding that Paramahansa Yogananda endeavored to awaken in those who sought his training. When difficulties arose in our personal lives or in the affairs of his worldwide society, we would hasten to him for a solution. However, it often happened that before we even had a chance to say anything, he would motion for us to sit and meditate. In his presence, our minds became calm and centered in God; and the restlessness and confusion created by our problems were completely dissolved. Even if he said nothing in answer to our questions, when we returned to our duties our thoughts formed more clearly, and we discovered that something within us had discerned the right way to proceed.

Paramahansaji gave us a solid grounding in the principles needed to guide our thoughts and actions with wisdom, courage, and faith. But he didn't do our thinking for us; he insisted that we develop our own discrimination by deepening our attunement with God, so that we could perceive for ourselves the best course of action in any particular situation.

It is my deepest hope that each reader will find in this sampling of Paramahansa Yogananda's words the wisdom and inspiration to chart a victorious path through the challenging circumstances of his or her own life. Above all, may these truths bring a lasting incentive to seek those inner resources of strength, joy, and love that spring from our eternal relationship with God. For in that discovery lies the highest fulfillment life can bring.

DAYA MATA

Los Angeles, California
December 1988

Introduction

"In seemingly empty space there is one Link, one Life eternal, which unites everything in the universe—animate and inanimate—one wave of Life flowing through everything."
— *Paramahansa Yogananda*

As our world civilization moves into the twenty-first century, our greatest cause for optimism is the emerging recognition of the underlying oneness of life. Humanity's loftiest spiritual traditions have taught for centuries that our lives are integral parts of a universal whole; today they are being joined by physicists, the new "visionaries," who are proclaiming that one cord of unity links the farthest galaxies with the smallest cells of our bodies. And as their findings begin to coalesce with those of biology, medicine, psychology, ecology, and other fields, we find ourselves poised on the brink of a revolution in human understanding — catching glimpses of a unity and harmony so vast, so breathtakingly perfect, that we are left with a radically different view of ourselves and our potentials.

This new vision offers a deep sense of reassurance in the face of the profound challenges confronting our world today. We are beginning to see that we are not helpless victims of a randomly chaotic cosmos. Diseases of body and mind; the equally alarming "dis-eases" affecting our family, social, and economic stability; the ecological threats to the earth itself — all these arise from a lack of accord with the essential harmony and unity of the cosmos, whether on the personal, community, national, or planetary level. By learning to integrate

our lives with this universal harmony, we can vic-
toriously meet any challenge to our well-being.*

Our age has been the recipient of an unprecedented
number of theories and methods for achieving that well-
being. Medicine, psychology, and the burgeoning number of metaphysical approaches all offer solutions from
their specialized perspectives; but the resulting ava-
lanche of information, much of it seemingly contra-
dictory, often leaves us unable to discern a continuity,
an order that gives focus to our efforts to help ourselves
and others. We find ourselves yearning for a larger perspective, some way of harmonizing and transcending the
partial views resulting from our era's overspecialization.

That larger perspective — anciently discovered by
the founders of the world's great spiritual traditions and
newly glimpsed by pioneering scientists of modern
times — reveals that underlying both science and religion are universal principles that govern all creation.
"Science looks at truth only from without," Paramahansa Yogananda said. "The metaphysician looks at
truth from within to without. That is why they clash.
But realized souls who understand science as well as
metaphysics find no difference at all. They see the par-

---

* "The cosmic order that upholds the universe is not different from
the moral order that rules man's destiny," wrote Paramahansa
Yogananda. Modern science is increasingly confirming the efficacy of
India's ancient methods of bringing human consciousness into
balanced harmony with cosmic laws, as evidenced by this recent
comment from Professor Brian D. Josephson, winner of the Nobel
Prize in physics: "The Vedanta and Sankhya [systems of Hindu philosophy of which Yoga is the practical application] hold the key to
the laws of mind and thought process, which are correlated to the
quantum field, i.e. the operation and distribution of particles at
atomic and molecular levels."

allelism between science and truth because they see the whole picture."

Paramahansa Yogananda's lifework* was to show how each of us can transform that vision of harmony from an intellectual possibility into direct personal experience that is applicable to our daily lives. A world teacher who brought the ancient science of yoga meditation† to the West in 1920, he dedicated his life to uniting East and West in the lasting ties of spiritual understanding, and to helping others toward realization of the infinite resources of peace, love, and joy that exist within every human being.

Where There Is Light contains but a small sampling of his teachings. The diverse flavor of its contents reflects the wide spectrum of sources from which they are drawn: Some passages are taken from public lectures or classes; others come from informal talks to small groups of disciples and friends; additional selections are from his writings.

A more detailed discussion of the principles referred to in the present volume can be found in the publications listed on page 183. For readers unfamiliar with the philosophy and spiritual ideals of Paramahansa Yogananda, *Where There Is Light* will serve as a useful introduction. And for all who have begun the inner journey toward the Source of that light, this compilation is offered as a handbook of spiritual counsel — a unique resource of insight and inspiration for daily life.

SELF-REALIZATION FELLOWSHIP

* See "About the Author," page 179.
† See *yoga* in glossary.

WHERE THERE IS LIGHT

CHAPTER 1

Our Infinite Potential

When we begin to understand the total being that is man, we realize that he is no simple physical organism. Within him are many powers whose potential he employs in greater or lesser degree in accommodating himself to the conditions of this world. Their potential is vastly greater than the average person thinks.

❖ ❖ ❖

Behind the light in every little bulb is a great dynamic current; beneath every little wave is the vast ocean, which has become the many waves. So it is with human beings. God made every man in His image,* and gave each one freedom. But you forget the Source of your being and the unequaled power of God that is an inherent part of you. The possibilities of this world are limitless; the potential progress of man is limitless.

❖ ❖ ❖

The real You is the prolific Source of all power; but the everyday you is only a fragment of that which can be brought out and manifested. The basic You is infinite in its potentiality.

❖ ❖ ❖

* Genesis 1:27.

3

What you are is much greater than anything or anyone else you have ever yearned for. God is manifest in you in a way that He is not manifest in any other human being. Your face is unlike anyone else's, your soul is unlike anyone else's, you are sufficient unto yourself; for within your soul lies the greatest treasure of all—God.

❖ ❖ ❖

All great teachers declare that within this body is the immortal soul, a spark of That which sustains all.

❖ ❖ ❖

Whence does our true personality derive? It comes from God. He is Absolute Consciousness, Absolute Existence, and Absolute Bliss . . . . By concentrating within, you can directly feel the divine bliss of your soul within and also without. If you can stabilize yourself in that consciousness, your outer personality will develop and become attractive to all beings. The soul is made in God's image, and when we become established in soul awareness, our personality begins to reflect His goodness and beauty. That is your real personality. Any other characteristics you display are more or less a graft—they are not the real "you."

❖ ❖ ❖

The urge to do and be that which is the noblest, the most beautiful of which we are capable, is the creative impulse of every high achievement. We strive for perfection here because we long to be restored to our oneness with God.

❖ ❖ ❖

The soul is absolutely perfect, but when identified with the body as ego,* its expression becomes distorted by human imperfections....Yoga teaches us to know the divine nature in ourselves and others. Through yoga meditation we can know that we are gods.†

❖ ❖ ❖

The moon's reflection cannot be seen clearly in ruffled water, but when the water's surface is calm a perfect reflection of the moon appears. So with the mind: when it is calm you see clearly reflected the moonèd face of the soul. As souls we are reflections of God. When by meditation techniques‡ we withdraw restless thoughts from the lake of the mind, we behold our soul, a perfect reflection of Spirit, and realize that the soul and God are One.

❖ ❖ ❖

Self-realization§ is the knowing—in body, mind, and soul—that we are one with the omnipresence of

---

* See *egoism* in glossary.

† "I have said, Ye are gods; and all of you are children of the Most High" (Psalms 82:6). "Is it not written in your law, I said, Ye are gods?" (John 10:34).

‡ "Be still, and know that I am God" (Psalms 46:10). Scientific techniques of yoga meditation that enable one to calm and interiorize the consciousness and perceive God's presence within are taught by Paramahansa Yogananda in *Self-Realization Fellowship Lessons*, a comprehensive home-study series compiled from his classes and lectures and available from Self-Realization Fellowship International Headquarters.

§ See *Self* in glossary.

God; that we do not have to pray that it come to us, that we are not merely near it at all times, but that God's omnipresence is our omnipresence; that we are just as much a part of Him now as we ever will be. All we have to do is improve our knowing.

❖ ❖ ❖

Focus your attention within.* You will feel a new power, a new strength, a new peace — in body, mind and spirit . . . . By communing with God you change your status from a mortal being to an immortal being. When you do this, all bonds that limit you will be broken.

❖ ❖ ❖

Mines of power lie unexplored within you. You use this power unconsciously in all things you do, and you achieve certain results; but, if you learn how to consciously control and use the powers within you, you can accomplish much more.

❖ ❖ ❖

Few people in this world try consciously to develop the potentials of body, mind, and soul. The rest are victims of circumstances of the past. They plod on and on, pushed by past wrong habits, helplessly going down under their influence, remembering only: "I am a nervous man," or "I am a weakling," or "I am a sinner," and so on.

* Neither shall they say, Lo here! or; lo there! for, behold, the kingdom of God is within you" (Luke 17:21).

It lies with each one of us to cut with the sword of wisdom the cords of our bondage, or to remain bound.

❖ ❖ ❖

One of the illusions of life is to continue to live helplessly. As soon as you say, "It's no use," it becomes so ....To think you cannot change at will is delusion.

❖ ❖ ❖

Our little minds are part of the omnipotent mind of God. Beneath the wave of our consciousness is the infinite ocean of His consciousness. It is because the wave forgets it is a part of the Ocean that it becomes isolated from that oceanic power. As a result, our minds have become weakened by our trials and material limitations. The mind has stopped its work. You will be surprised how much it can do if you cast off the limitations you have put on it.

❖ ❖ ❖

Why limit your capability to the adage, "Don't bite off more than you can chew"? I believe you should bite off more than you can chew, and then chew it!

❖ ❖ ❖

The mind is like an elastic band. The more you pull, the more it stretches. The mind-elastic will never break. Every time you feel limitations, close your eyes and say to yourself, "I am the Infinite," and you will see what power you have.

❖ ❖ ❖

When you say to me that you can't do this or
that, I don't believe it. Whatever you make up your
mind to do, you can do. God is the sum total of everything, and His image is within you. He can do anything, and so can you, if you learn to identify yourself
with His inexhaustible nature.

❖ ❖ ❖

Don't look on yourself as a weak mortal. Incredible amounts of energy are hidden in your brain; enough
in a gram of flesh to run the city of Chicago for two
days.* And you say you are tired?

❖ ❖ ❖

God made us angels of energy, encased in solids
—currents of life dazzling through a material bulb of
flesh. But through concentration on the frailties and
fragility of the body bulb, we have forgotten how to
feel the immortal, indestructible properties of the
eternal life energy within the mutable flesh.

❖ ❖ ❖

When you go beyond the consciousness of this
world, knowing that you are not the body or the mind,
and yet aware as never before that you exist — that
divine consciousness is what you are. You are That in
which is rooted everything in the universe.

❖ ❖ ❖

* Centuries before modern physicists proved the equivalence of matter and energy, India's sages proclaimed that every material form is
reducible to patterns of energy. See *prana* in glossary.

You are all gods, if you only knew it. Behind the wave of your consciousness is the sea of God's presence. You must look within. Don't concentrate on the little wave of the body with its weaknesses; look beneath....As you lift your consciousness from the body and its experiences, you will find that sphere [of your consciousness] filled with the great joy and bliss that lights the stars and gives power to the winds and storms. God is the source of all our joys and of all the manifestations in nature....

Awaken yourself from the gloom of ignorance. You have closed your eyes in the sleep of delusion.* Awake! Open your eyes and you shall behold the glory of God — the vast vista of God's light spreading over all things. I am telling you to be divine realists, and you will find the answer to all questions in God.

Affirmations†

I am submerged in eternal light. It permeates every particle of my being. I am living in that light. The Divine Spirit fills me within and without.

❖ ❖ ❖

O Father, break the boundaries of the little waves of my life that I may join the ocean of Thy vastness.

---

* See *maya* in glossary.
† Instructions for using affirmations are given on pages 28 ff.

CHAPTER 2

Strength in Times of Adversity

Everything the Lord has created is to try us, to bring out the buried soul immortality within us. That is the adventure of life, the one purpose of life. And everyone's adventure is different, unique. You should be prepared to deal with all problems of health, mind, and soul by commonsense methods and faith in God, knowing that in life or death your soul remains unconquered.

❖ ❖ ❖

Never let life beat you down. Beat life! If you have a strong will you can overcome all difficulties. Affirm, even in the midst of trials: "Danger and I were born together, and I am more dangerous than danger!" This is a truth you should always remember; apply it and you will see that it works. Don't behave like a cringing mortal being. You are a child of God!

❖ ❖ ❖

Many people are afraid of life's problems. I have never feared them, for I have always prayed: "Lord, may Thy power increase in me. Keep me in the positive consciousness that with Thy help I can always overcome my difficulties."

❖ ❖ ❖

Since you are made in God's image, to believe that your tests are more difficult than your divinity is powerful to overcome them is to believe in an untruth. Remember, no matter what your tests are, you are not too weak to fight. God will not suffer you to be tempted more than you are able to bear.

❖ ❖ ❖

Saint Francis had more troubles than you could imagine, but he didn't give up. One by one, by the power of mind, he overcame those obstacles and became one with the Master of the Universe. Why shouldn't you have that kind of determination?

❖ ❖ ❖

Use every trial that comes to you as an opportunity to improve yourself. When you are passing through the difficulties and tests of life, you usually become rebellious: "Why should this happen to me?" Instead, you should think of every trial as a pickax with which to dig into the soil of your consciousness and release the fountain of spiritual strength that lies within. Each test should bring out the hidden power that is within you as a child of God, made in His image.

❖ ❖ ❖

To fly away from problems may seem the easiest solution. But you gain strength only when you wrestle with a strong opponent. One who doesn't have difficulties is one who doesn't grow.

❖ ❖ ❖

Life is worth nothing if it is not a continuous overcoming of problems. Each problem that waits for a solution at your hand is a religious duty imposed upon you by life itself. Any escape from problems, physical or mental, is an escape from life, as there can be no life that is not full of problems.

❖ ❖ ❖

Meet everybody and every circumstance on the battlefield of life with the courage of a hero and the smile of a conqueror.

❖ ❖ ❖

When my trials become very great, I first seek understanding in myself. I don't blame circumstances or try to correct anybody else. I go inside first. I try to clean the citadel of my soul to remove anything that obstructs the soul's all-powerful, all-wise expression. That is the successful way to live.

❖ ❖ ❖

Trouble and disease have a lesson for us. Our painful experiences are not meant to destroy us, but to burn out our dross, to hurry us back Home. No one is more anxious for our release than God.

❖ ❖ ❖

The smoke-screen of delusion has come between us and God, and He is sorry that we have lost sight of Him. He is not happy seeing His children suffer so much — dying from falling bombs, terrible diseases, and wrong habits of living. He regrets it, for He loves us and wants us back. If only you would make the effort at night to meditate and be with Him! He thinks of you so much. You are not forsaken. It is you who have forsaken your Self.

❖ ❖ ❖

When you use life's experiences as your teacher, and learn from them the true nature of the world and your part in it, those experiences become valuable guides to eternal fulfillment and happiness.

❖ ❖ ❖

In a sense misery is your best friend, because it starts you seeking God. When you begin to see clearly the imperfection of the world, you will begin to seek the perfection of God. The truth is that God is using evil, not to destroy us, but to make us disillusioned with His toys, with the playthings of this world, so that we might seek Him.

❖ ❖ ❖

Gloom is but the shade of Divine Mother's* hand outstretched caressingly. Don't forget that. Sometimes, when the Mother is going to caress you, a shadow is caused by Her hand before it touches you. So when trouble comes, don't think that She is punishing you; Her hand overshadowing you holds some blessing as it reaches out to bring you nearer to Her.

❖ ❖ ❖

Suffering is a good teacher to those who are quick and willing to learn from it. But it becomes a tyrant to those who resist and resent. Suffering can teach us al-

---

* The scriptures of India teach that God is both personal and impersonal, immanent and transcendent. Seekers in the West have traditionally related to God in His personal aspect as Father; in India, the concept of God as the loving, compassionate Mother of the Universe has widespread appeal. See *Divine Mother* in glossary.

most everything. Its lessons urge us to develop discrimination, self-control, nonattachment, morality,
and transcendent spiritual consciousness. For example, a stomachache tells us not to eat too much and
to watch what we eat. The pain from loss of possessions or loved ones reminds us of the temporal nature
of all things in this world of delusion. The conse-
quences of wrong actions impel us to exercise discrimination. Why not learn through wisdom? Then
you won't subject yourself to unnecessary painful discipline from the hard taskmaster of suffering.

❖ ❖ ❖

Suffering is caused by the misuse of free will. God
has given us the power to accept Him or reject Him. He
doesn't want us to encounter woes, but will not inter-
fere when we choose actions that lead to misery.

❖ ❖ ❖

All the causes of ill health or sudden financial
failure or other troubles that come upon you without
warning, and without your knowing why, were created by you in the past, in this or in previous incarnations, and have been silently germinating in your
consciousness.... * Don't blame God or anyone else
if you are suffering from disease, financial problems,

---

* Reincarnation, the soul's evolutionary journey back to God,
provides repeated opportunities for growth, achievement, and fulfillment not possible in one brief lifespan of earthly existence. See
glossary.

emotional upsets. You created the cause of the problem in the past and must make a greater determination to uproot it now.

❖ ❖ ❖

Too many people misinterpret the meaning of karma,* adopting a fatalistic attitude. You do not have to accept karma. If I tell you that somebody is standing behind you ready to hurt you because you once hit him, and you meekly say, "Well, it is my karma," and wait for him to strike you, of course you will get a blow! Why don't you try to mollify him? By pacifying him you may lessen his bitterness and remove his desire to strike you.

❖ ❖ ❖

The effects of your actions have much less power to hurt you when you do not allow the mind to give in to them. Remember that. You can also resist by counteracting the bad effects of past wrong actions with good effects set in motion by present right actions, thus preventing the creation of an environment favorable to the fruition of your bad karma.

❖ ❖ ❖

When you realize yourself as a child of God, what karma have you? God has no karma. And you have none, when you *know* you are His child. Every day you should affirm, "I am not a mortal being; I am not the body. I am a child of God." That is practicing the

* The results of past actions, governed by the law of cause and effect. "Whatsoever a man soweth, that shall he also reap" (Galatians 6:7). See glossary.

presence of God. God is free from karma. You are made in His image. You also are free from karma.

❖ ❖ ❖

Let nobody tell you your suffering or problems are your karma. You [the soul] have no karma. Shankara* said: "I am one with Spirit; I am He." If you *realize* this truth, you are a god. But if you keep mentally affirming, "I am a god," and in the background of your mind you are thinking, "But it seems I am a mortal being," you are a mortal being. If you *know* you are a god, you are free.

❖ ❖ ❖

"Know ye not that ye are the temple of God, and that the Spirit of God dwelleth in you?"† If you can clarify and expand your mind through meditation, and receive God in your consciousness, you too will be free from the delusion of disease, limitations, and death.

❖ ❖ ❖

If you want to rise above karma, try to realize these three truths: (1) *When the mind is strong and the heart is pure, you are free.* It is the mind that connects you with pain in the body. When you think pure thoughts and are mentally strong, you cannot suffer the painful effects of evil karma. This is something very cheerful I have found. (2) *In subconscious sleep,*

* Swami Shankara was one of India's most illustrious philosophers. His date is uncertain; many scholars assign him to the ninth century.
† I Corinthians 3:16.

you are free. (3) *When you are in ecstasy,* * *identified with God, you have no karma.* This is why the saints say, "Pray unceasingly." When you continuously pray and meditate, you go into the land of superconsciousness, where no troubles can reach you.

❖ ❖ ❖

You can be free from karma right now, by these methods. Whenever karmic troubles plague you, go to sleep. Or, think pure thoughts and make the mind like steel, saying to yourself: "I am above it all." Or, best of all, in deep meditation go into the divine state of superconsciousness. The bliss of that consciousness is the natural state of your soul, but you have forgotten your real nature by being so long identified with the body. That untroubled, blissful state of the soul has to be reacquired.

❖ ❖ ❖

The soul's nature [as individualized Spirit] is bliss: a lasting, inner state of ever-new, ever-changing joy. This bliss eternally gives unfading joy to one who attains it, even when he is passing through trials of physical suffering or death.

❖ ❖ ❖

Material remedies — medicines, physical comforts, human consolation — have their place in help-

* The elevated state of consciousness in which there is direct experience of God. The conscious state is awareness of the body and its external environment. The subconscious state is the inner mind, operative in sleep and such mental processes as memory. The superconscious state is the transcendent higher mind or spiritual consciousness of the soul. See glossary.

ing to remove pain, but the greatest remedy is the practice of *Kriya Yoga** and the affirmation that you are one with God. This is the cure-all for every trouble, pain, and bereavement—the way to freedom from all individual and mass karma.†

Affirmations

I know that God's power is limitless; and as I am made in His image, I, too, have the strength to overcome all obstacles.

❖ ❖ ❖

Dear Father, whatever conditions confront me, I know that they represent the next step in my unfoldment. I will welcome all tests because I know that within me is the intelligence to understand and the power to overcome.

---

* A scientific technique of interiorized God-communion. The science of Kriya Yoga is explained in Paramahansa Yogananda's *Autobiography of a Yogi.* See glossary.

† The cumulative actions of human beings within communities, nations, or the world as a whole constitute mass karma, which produces local or far-ranging effects according to the degree and preponderance of good or evil. The thoughts and actions of every individual, therefore, contribute to the good or ill of this world and all peoples in it.

CHAPTER 3

Rising Above Suffering

I have had continual controversy with my Heavenly Father as to why pain is a test to bring back to Him human beings who are made in His image. I tell the Father that in pain there is a compulsion; persuasion and love are better ways to get human beings back to heaven. Even though I know the answer, I have always fought with God on these points, for He understands me as a father understands his son.

❖ ❖ ❖

How tragic is this world! It is a place of uncertainty. But no matter what has happened to you, if you throw yourself at the feet of the Father and seek His mercy, He will lift you up and show you that life is but a dream.*

❖ ❖ ❖

I will tell you a little story. A king fell asleep and dreamed that he was poor. He was crying out in his sleep for just a penny for some food. Finally, the queen woke him and said, "What is the matter with you? Your treasury is full of gold, and yet you are crying for a penny."

Then the king said, "Oh, how silly of me. I thought I was a beggar and was starving for lack of that penny."

Such is the delusion of every soul who is dream-

---

* See *maya* in glossary.

ing he is a mortal, subject to the nightmarish evils of all kinds of disease, suffering, troubles, heartbreaks. The only way to escape this nightmare is by becoming more attached to God and less attached to the dream images of this world.

❖ ❖ ❖

No cruelty exists in God's plan, because in His eyes there is no good or evil—only pictures of light and shadows. The Lord intended us to view the dualistic scenes of life as He does Himself—the ever joyous Witness of a stupendous cosmic drama.

Man has falsely identified himself with the pseudo-soul or ego. When he transfers his sense of identity to his true being, the immortal soul, he discovers that all pain is unreal. He no longer can even *imagine* the state of suffering.

❖ ❖ ❖

The superconsciousness of man is made of God and is painproof. All physical and mental sufferings come by identification, imagination, and wrong human habits of thinking.

❖ ❖ ❖

Have more mental strength. Develop such mental power that you can stand unshaken, no matter what comes, bravely facing anything in life. If you love God you should have faith and be prepared to endure when trials come. Don't be afraid of suffering. Keep your mind positive and strong. It is your inner experience that is most important.

❖ ❖ ❖

You heighten suffering by imagination. Worrying or feeling sorry for yourself won't ease your pain, but rather increase it. For instance, someone wrongs you; you dwell on it, and your friends talk about it and sympathize with you. The more you think of it, the more you magnify the hurt— *and* your suffering.

❖ ❖ ❖

Some people go on remembering all the suffering they passed through, and how terrible the pain was, from an operation that took place twenty years ago! Over and over again they relive the consciousness of that sickness. Why repeat such experiences?

❖ ❖ ❖

The best way to dissociate yourself from your difficulty is to be mentally detached, as if you were merely a spectator, while at the same time seeking a remedy.*

❖ ❖ ❖

The fact is, if you learn to live in your body without thinking of it as yourself, you won't suffer so much. The connection between you and bodily pain is only mental. When you are asleep and unconscious of the body, you feel no pain. Likewise, when a doctor or a dentist gives you an anesthetic and performs surgery on your body, you don't feel any pain. The mind has been disconnected from the sensation.

❖ ❖ ❖

Look after the body, but be above it. Know that

* Persons with serious or persistent health problems—pain or other symptoms—should follow the advice of a medical doctor.

you are separate from your mortal form. Put up a great mental barrier between your mind and body. Affirm: "I am apart from the body. No heat, cold, or sickness can touch me. I am free." Your limitations will become less and less.

❖ ❖ ❖

The best anesthesia against pain is your mental power. If your mind refuses to accept it, pain will be greatly lessened. I have seen, at times when this body got hurt and felt severe pain, that if I put my mind at the Christ center* —that is, if I identify myself more with God and less with the body — there is no pain at all. So when pain comes, concentrate at the Christ center. Be mentally apart from pain; develop more strength of mind. Be tough within. When you are feeling pain, inwardly say to yourself, "It doesn't hurt me." When a hurt comes, recognize it as something to be cared for, but don't suffer over it. The more you concentrate on the power of the mind, the more your body consciousness drops away.

❖ ❖ ❖

"Pain and pleasure are transitory," [Sri Yukteswar† told his disciples]. "Endure all dualities with calm-

* The seat of the singular eye of divine consciousness and spiritual perception at the point between the eyebrows, of which Jesus spoke when he said: "If therefore thine eye be single, thy whole body shall be full of light" (Matthew 6:22). Pictures of saints in divine communion often show them with with their eyes thus upturned to this center. See glossary.

† Swami Sri Yukteswar (1855–1936) was the guru (spiritual preceptor) of Paramahansa Yogananda. His life is described in the latter's *Autobiography of a Yogi*. See glossary.

ness, trying at the same time to remove yourself beyond their power."

❖ ❖ ❖

In the midst of negative conditions, practice "opposition" by thinking and acting in a positive, constructive way. Practice *titiksha,** which means not to give in to unpleasant experiences, but to resist them without becoming upset mentally. When sickness comes, follow hygienic laws of living, without permitting your mind to be disturbed. Be unruffled in everything you do.

❖ ❖ ❖

Whether you are suffering in this life, or smiling with opulence and power, your consciousness should remain unchanged. If you can accomplish even-mindedness, nothing can ever hurt you. The lives of all great masters show that they have achieved this blessed state.

❖ ❖ ❖

Meditation is the way by which you must strive to rise above delusion and know your true nature. If you can hold on to that consciousness in activity as well as in meditation, remaining undisturbed by delusive experiences, then you will be above this dream world of God's. The dream will be over for you. This is why Lord Krishna† stressed that if you want freedom in Spirit, you must be of even mind under all cir-

* Sanskrit, "endurance with mental evenness."
† An avatar (divine incarnation) who lived in India three millenniums before the Christian era. Lord Krishna's discourse to the disciple Arjuna on the battlefield of Kurukshetra forms the immortal scripture, Bhagavad Gita. See *Bhagavan Krishna* and *Bhagavad Gita* in glossary.

cumstances: "The man who is calm and even-minded during pain and pleasure, the one whom these cannot ruffle, he alone is fit to attain everlastingness."[*]

❖ ❖ ❖

When tigers of worries, sickness, and death are chasing you, your only sanctuary is the inner temple of silence. The spiritually deep man lives day and night in a calm interior silence into which neither menacing worries nor even the crash of colliding worlds can intrude.

❖ ❖ ❖

No sensation or mental torture can affect you if the mind is dissociated from it and anchored in the peace and joy of God.

The Healing Power of God

There are two ways in which our needs can be taken care of. One is the material. For example, when we have ill health we can go to a doctor for medical treatment. But a time comes when no human aid can help. Then we look to the other way, to the Spiritual Power, the Maker of our body, mind, and soul. Material power is limited, and when it fails, we turn to the unlimited Divine Power. Likewise with our financial needs; when we have done our best, and still it is inadequate, we turn to that other Power.

❖ ❖ ❖

To know God is the most important way to heal

[*] Bhagavad Gita II:15.

all disease—physical, mental, spiritual. As darkness cannot remain where light is, so also the darkness of disease is driven away by the light of God's perfect presence when it enters the body.

❖ ❖ ❖

The unlimited power of God is working behind all methods of healing, whether physical, mental, or vital.* This fact must never be forgotten, for if one depends upon the *method* and not upon *God*, he automatically hinders and limits the free flow of the healing power.

❖ ❖ ❖

Your duty is to bring your need to God's attention, and to do your part in helping God to bring that desire to fruition. For example, in chronic diseases, do your best to help promote healing, but know in your mind that ultimately God alone can help.

❖ ❖ ❖

An unlimited source of protection for man lies in his strong thought that, as a child of God, he cannot be affected by disease.

❖ ❖ ❖

Do your best to remove the causes of illness and then be absolutely unafraid. There are so many germs everywhere that if you began to fear them you would not be able to enjoy life at all.... Be fearless.

* "Vital" healing refers to tapping the cosmic energy—the intelligent, finer-than-atomic energy—that is the universal life-principle through which God sustains all creation. See *prana* in glossary.

❖ ❖ ❖

Keep smiling within, pulsating with deep joy, ever ready to act, and spiritually ambitious to help others. These attitudes are not only good exercises for the mind; they also keep the body constantly supplied with fresh cosmic energy.

❖ ❖ ❖

He who finds joy within himself discovers that his body is charged with electric current, life energy, not from food but from God. If you feel that you can't smile, stand before a mirror and with your fingers pull your mouth into a smile. It is that important!...

When one is joyful within, he invites the help of the inexhaustible power of God. I mean a sincere joyfulness, not that which you feign outwardly but do not feel within. When your joy is sincere you are a smile-millionaire. A genuine smile distributes the cosmic current, *prana*, to every body cell. The happy man is less subject to disease, for happiness actually attracts into the body a greater supply of the universal life energy.

❖ ❖ ❖

In the vault of the mind lie all the chains of bondage, as well as the keys to freedom.

❖ ❖ ❖

Mind power carries with it the unfailing energy of God; that is the power you want in your body. And there is a way to bring in that power. The way is communion with God by meditation. When your communion with Him is perfect, the healing is permanent.

The Power of Affirmation and Prayer

In the past you may have been disappointed that your prayers were not answered. But do not lose faith. ...God is not a mute unfeeling Being. He is love itself. If you know how to meditate to make contact with Him, He will respond to your loving demands.

❖ ❖ ❖

To know exactly how and when to pray, according to the nature of our needs, is what brings the desired results. When the right method is applied, it sets in motion the proper laws of God; the operation of these laws scientifically bears results.

❖ ❖ ❖

The first rule in prayer is to approach God only with legitimate desires. The second is to pray for their fulfillment, not as a beggar, but as a son: "I am Thy child. Thou art my Father. Thou and I are One." When you pray deeply and continuously you will feel a great joy welling up in your heart. Don't be satisfied until that joy manifests; for when you feel that all-satisfying joy in your heart, you will know that God has tuned in your prayer broadcast. Then pray to your Father: "Lord, this is my need. I am willing to work for it; please guide me and help me to have the right thoughts and to do the right things to bring about success. I will use my reason, and work with determination, but guide Thou my reason, will, and activity to the right thing that I should do."

❖ ❖ ❖

You should pray to God intimately, as His child, which you are. God does not object when you pray from your ego, as a stranger and a beggar, but you will find that your efforts are limited by that consciousness. God does not want you to give up your own will power, which is your divine birthright as His child.

❖ ❖ ❖

An unceasing demand* for anything, mentally whispered with unflagging zeal and unflinching courage and faith, develops into a dynamic power that so influences the entire behavior of the conscious, subconscious, and superconscious powers of man that the desired object is gained. The inner performance of mental whispers must be unceasing, undaunted by reverses. Then the desired-for object will materialize.

Technique of Affirmation

The infinite potencies of sound derive from the Creative Word, *Aum*,† the cosmic vibratory power behind all atomic energies. Any word spoken with clear realization and deep concentration has a materializing value.

❖ ❖ ❖

* Paramahansa Yogananda taught: "Prayer often implies the consciousness of beggary. We are children of God, not beggars, and are thus entitled to our divine inheritance. When we have established a connection of love between our souls and God, we have a right to lovingly *demand* the fulfillment of our legitimate prayers." This principle of demanding our birthright from God is the enlivening power within an affirmation.

† The great Amen or "Word of God." See *Aum* in glossary.

Words saturated with sincerity, conviction, faith, and intuition are like highly explosive vibration bombs, which, when set off, shatter the rocks of difficulties and create the change desired.

❖ ❖ ❖

The subconscious idea-habit of disease or health exerts a strong influence. Stubborn mental or physical diseases always have a deep root in the subconsciousness. Illness may be cured by pulling out its hidden roots. That is why all affirmations of the conscious mind should be *impressive* enough to permeate the subconsciousness, which in turn automatically influences the conscious mind. Strong conscious affirmations thus react on the mind and body through the medium of the subconsciousness. Still stronger affirmations reach not only the subconscious but also the superconscious mind — the magic storehouse of miraculous powers.

❖ ❖ ❖

Patience and attentive, intelligent repetition are wonder-workers. Affirmations for curing chronic mental or bodily afflictions should be repeated often,* deeply and continuously (utterly ignoring unchanged or contrary conditions, if any), until they become part of one's profound intuitional convictions.

❖ ❖ ❖

* Affirmations for specific purposes are given at the end of each chapter in this book. In *Scientific Healing Affirmations, Metaphysical Meditations,* and *Self-Realization Lessons,* Paramahansa Yogananda provides hundreds of other affirmations for healing, self-improvement, and deepening one's awareness of God.

Choose your affirmation and repeat all of it, first loudly, then softly and more slowly, until your voice becomes a whisper. Then gradually affirm it mentally only, without moving the tongue or the lips, until you feel that you have attained deep, unbroken concentration — not unconsciousness, but a profound continuity of uninterrupted thought.

If you continue with your mental affirmation, and go still deeper, you will feel a sense of increasing joy and peace. During the state of deep concentration, your affirmation will merge with the subconscious stream, to come back later reinforced with power to influence your conscious mind through the law of habit.

During the time that you experience ever increasing peace, your affirmation goes deeper, into the superconscious realm, to return later laden with unlimited power to influence your conscious mind and also to fulfill your desires. Doubt not and you shall witness the miracle of this scientific faith.

❖ ❖ ❖

Blind repetition of demands or affirmations, without concomitant devotion or spontaneous love, makes one merely a "praying victrola," which does not know what its prayer means. Grinding out prayers vocally and mechanically, while inwardly thinking of something else, does not bring response from God. A blind repetition, taking the name of God in vain, is fruitless. Repeating a demand or prayer over and over again, mentally or orally, and with deepening attention and devotion, spiritualizes the prayer, and changes conscious, believing repetition into superconscious experience.

❖ ❖ ❖

Meditate on the meaning of the demand you have selected, until it becomes a part of you. Saturate the demand with devotion as you meditate upon it. As your meditation becomes deeper, increase your devotion and mentally offer the demand as your own heart's outburst. Imbue yourself with faith that your heart's craving, expressed through this specific demand, is being felt by God.

Feel that just behind the screen of your devotional demand God is listening to the silent words of your soul. Feel this! Be one with your heart's demand — and be thoroughly convinced that He has listened to you. Then go about your duties, seeking not to know whether God will grant your demand. Believe absolutely that your demand has been heard, and that you will know that what is God's is yours also. Unceasingly meditate on God; and when you feel Him, you will acquire your rightful inheritance as His divine son.

❖ ❖ ❖

"The Lord responds to all and works for all," [Sri Yukteswar said]. "Seldom do men realize how often God heeds their prayers. He is not partial to a few, but listens to everyone who approaches Him trustfully. His children should ever have implicit faith in the loving-kindness of their Omnipresent Father."

❖ ❖ ❖

Faith has to be cultivated, or rather uncovered

within us. It is there but has to be brought out. If you watch your life you will see the innumerable ways in which God works through it; your faith will thus be strengthened. Few people look for His hidden hand. Most men consider the course of events as natural and inevitable. They little know what radical changes are possible through prayer!

Cultivating Faith in God

Absolute, unquestioning faith in God is the greatest method of instantaneous healing. An unceasing effort to arouse that faith is man's highest and most rewarding duty.

❖ ❖ ❖

Belief in God and faith in God are different. A belief is valueless if you don't test it and live by it. Belief converted into experience becomes faith.

❖ ❖ ❖

You may want to believe; you may even think you believe; but if you really believe, the result will be instantaneous.

❖ ❖ ❖

Faith cannot be contradicted: it is intuitive conviction of truth, and it cannot be shaken even by contrary evidence....You don't realize how wonderfully this great power works. It operates mathematically. There is no "if" about it. And that is what the Bible means by faith: it is *proof* of things unseen.*

* "Faith is the substance of things hoped for, the evidence of things not seen" (Hebrews 11:1).

❖ ❖ ❖

Always undoubtingly believe that God's power is working in you, just behind your thoughts, prayers, and convictions, to give infinite strength....Acknowledge His working within you in everything and you will have Him always with you.

❖ ❖ ❖

The Supreme Power may be invoked by continuous faith and unceasing prayer. You should eat rightly and do whatever else is necessary for the body, but continuously pray to Him: "Lord, Thou canst heal me because Thou dost control the life atoms and subtle conditions of the body that doctors cannot reach with medicines."

❖ ❖ ❖

In a voice resounding with joy, [Lahiri Mahasaya* said]: "Always know that the omnipotent Paramatman† can heal anyone, doctor or no doctor."

❖ ❖ ❖

This is God's world. He takes you; He keeps you. When the doctor says, "Well, I'll heal you," if God makes up His mind to take you, you will go. So live your life for Him.

❖ ❖ ❖

If a person falls ill he should earnestly try to rid himself of his malady. Then, even if doctors tell him there is no hope, he should remain tranquil, for by

* The guru of Paramahansa Yogananda's guru. See glossary.
† Sanskrit, "Supreme Spirit."

fear he shuts his eyes of faith to the unfailing Divine Presence. Instead of indulging in anxiety he should affirm: "I am ever safe in the fortress of Thy loving care." A fearless devotee, dying from an incurable disease, concentrates on the Lord and becomes ready for liberation in his next life....All men should realize that soul consciousness can triumph over all external disasters.

❖ ❖ ❖

Even death is nothing to the spiritually strong. I once dreamed I was dying. Nevertheless I was praying to Him: "Lord, it is all right; whatever is Thy will." Then He touched me and I realized the truth: "How can I die? The wave cannot die; it sinks back into the ocean and comes forth again. The wave never dies; and I can never die."

❖ ❖ ❖

[During a period of great trial, Paramahansa Yogananda retired to the desert for solitude and prayer. One night while deeply meditating, he received this beautiful response from God:]

"Dance of life or dance of death,
Know that these come from Me, and rejoice.
What more dost thou want, than that thou
          hast Me?"

❖ ❖ ❖

*[The exemplary lives of saintly souls are inexhaustible
sources of strength and inspiration to others. The right attitude toward suffering found perfect expression in the life
of Sri Gyanamata (1869–1951),* one of the foremost disciples of Paramahansa Yogananda. All who knew her were
uplifted by her quiet heroism, her inner strength and love
for God that never wavered despite the great physical
suffering she endured for the last two decades of her life.
During the memorial service for her conducted by Paramahansaji, he spoke these words:]*

Sister's life has been like that of St. Francis, who
suffered even while helping others. So she stands as
a great inspiration. In all those years she suffered, she
showed that her love for God was greater; and I never
saw one mark of that suffering in her eyes. That is
why she is a great saint — a great soul — and that is
why she is with God....

When I looked at her body in the casket, I felt
Sister's soul commingled with the omnipresent ether,
and I heard the voice of the Father speaking to me
from within: "Twenty years of suffering never took
away her love from Me, and that is what I prize in her
life." I could not say anything more; I realized that
the Heavenly Father has a right to test our love for
Him with pain, for even twenty years or more, in order that we may claim in exchange our lost eternal,
ever-new happiness as His image.

Then again I choked with the thrill of God's pres-

* Gyanamata means "Mother of Wisdom." Her wise and loving counsel and encouragement to others are beautifully expressed in the col-
lection of her letters and account of her life in *God Alone,* published
by Self-Realization Fellowship.

ence, and I said to myself: "To regain the eternity of
ever new joy through twenty years of being unruffled
by pain is the greater achievement, through the grace
of the Father."

❖ ❖ ❖

If you live with the Lord, you will be healed of
the delusions of life and death, health and sickness.
Be in the Lord. Feel His love. Fear nothing. Only in
the castle of God can we find protection. There is no
safer haven of joy than in His presence. When you are
with Him, nothing can touch you.

Affirmations for Healing

*God's perfect health permeates the dark nooks
of my bodily sickness. In all my cells His healing light is shining. They are entirely well, for
His perfection is in them.*

❖ ❖ ❖

*The healing power of Spirit is flowing through
all the cells of my body. I am made of the one
universal God-substance.*

❖ ❖ ❖

*Thy perfect light is omnipresent in all my body
parts. Wherever that healing light is manifest,
there is perfection. I am well, for perfection is
in me.*

❖ ❖ ❖

*I am the Changeless, I am the Infinite. I am
not a little mortal being with bones to break,*

a body that will perish. I am the deathless, changeless Infinite.

❖ ❖ ❖

O Divine Mother, whether I float on the surface of the present life, or sink beneath the waves of death, I am held in Thine immortal arms.

CHAPTER 4

Security in
an Uncertain World

The sudden cataclysms that occur in nature, creating havoc and mass injury, are not "acts of God." Such disasters result from the thoughts and actions of man. Wherever the world's vibratory balance of good and evil is disturbed by an accumulation of harmful vibrations, the result of man's wrong thinking and wrong doing, you will see devastation....*

Wars are brought about not by fateful divine action but by widespread material selfishness. Banish selfishness—individual, industrial, political, national—and you will have no more wars.

❖ ❖ ❖

Modern chaotic conditions all over the world are the result of living by ungodly ideals. Individuals and nations can be protected from utter destruction if they live by heavenly ideals of brotherhood, industrial cooperation, and international exchange of earthly goods and experiences.

❖ ❖ ❖

I believe a time will come when in greater understanding we shall have no boundaries anymore. We shall call the earth our country; and we shall, by a

* See footnote on page 18.

process of justice and international assembly, distribute unselfishly the goods of the world according to the needs of the people. But equality cannot be established by force; it must come from the heart....We must start now, with ourselves. We should try to be like the divine ones who have come on earth again and again to show us the way. By our loving each other and keeping our understanding clear, as they taught and exemplified, peace can come.

❖ ❖ ❖

You may think it is hopeless to try to conquer hatred and inspire mankind to Christlike ways of love, but never was the need so great as now. Atheistic ideologies are battling to drive religion out. The world is marching on in a wild drama of existence. Trying to stop the raging storms, we seem no more than little ants swimming in the ocean. But do not minimize your power.

❖ ❖ ❖

The one thing that will help to eliminate world suffering — more than money, houses, or any other material aid — is to meditate and transmit to others the divine consciousness of God that we feel. A thousand dictators could never destroy what I have within. Every day radiate His consciousness to others. Try to understand God's plan for mankind — to draw all souls back to Himself — and work in harmony with His will.

❖ ❖ ❖

God is Love; His plan for creation can be rooted only in love. Does not that simple thought, rather than erudite reasonings, offer solace to the human heart? Every saint who has penetrated to the core of Reality has testified that a divine universal plan exists and that it is beautiful and full of joy.

❖ ❖ ❖

As soon as we learn in meditation to love God, we shall love all mankind as we love our own family. Those who have found God through their own Self-realization—those who have actually experienced God — they alone *can* love mankind; not impersonally, but as their blood brothers, children of the same one Father.

❖ ❖ ❖

Realize that the same lifeblood is circulating in the veins of all races. How may anyone dare to hate any other human being, of whatever race, when God lives and breathes in all? We are Americans or Hindus or other nationalities for just a few years, but we are God's children forever. The soul cannot be confined within man-made boundaries. Its nationality is Spirit; its country is Omnipresence.

❖ ❖ ❖

If you contact God within yourself, you will know that He is in everyone, that He has become the children of all races. Then you cannot be an enemy to anyone. If the whole world could love with that universal love, there would be no need for men to arm themselves against one another. By our own Christ-like example we must bring unity among all reli-gions, all nations, all races.

❖ ❖ ❖

The broad sympathies and discerning insight need-ed for the healing of earthly woes cannot flow from a mere intellectual consideration of human diversities, but from knowledge of men's deepest unity—kinship with God. Toward realization of the world's highest ideal — peace through brotherhood — may Yoga, the science of personal communion with the Divine, spread in time to all men in all lands.

❖ ❖ ❖

The grim march of world political events points inexorably to the truth that without spiritual vision, the people perish. Science, if not religion, has awak-ened in humanity a dim sense of the insecurity and even insubstantiality of all material things. Where in-deed may man go now, if not to his Source and Origin, the Spirit within him?

❖ ❖ ❖

The Atomic Age will see men's minds sobered and broadened by the now scientifically indisputable truth that matter is in reality a concentrate of energy. The human mind can and must liberate within itself energies greater than those within stones and metals, lest the material atomic giant, newly unleashed, turn on the world in mindless destruction. An indirect benefit of mankind's concern over atomic bombs may be an increased practical interest in the science of Yoga, a "bombproof shelter" truly.

❖ ❖ ❖

This world will always have turmoil and trouble. What are you worried about? Go to the shelter of God, where the Masters have gone, and whence they are watching and helping the world. You shall have safety forever, not only for yourself, but for all those loved ones who have been entrusted to your care by our Lord and Father.

❖ ❖ ❖

True happiness, lasting happiness, lies only in God, "having whom no other gain is greater."* In Him is the only safety, the only shelter, the only escape from all our fears. You have no other security in the world, no other freedom. The only true freedom lies in God. So strive deeply to contact Him in meditation morning and night, as well as throughout the day in all work and duties you perform. Yoga teaches that where God is, there is no fear, no sorrow. The successful yogi† can stand unshaken 'midst the crash of breaking worlds; he is secure in the realization: "Lord, where I am, there Thou must come."

❖ ❖ ❖

Don't be attached to the passing dreams of life. Live for God and God alone. This is the only way to have freedom and safety in this world. Outside of God

* Paraphrase of Bhagavad Gita VI:22.
† See glossary.

there is no security; no matter where you go, delusion can attack you. Be free right now. Be a son of God now; realize you are His child, so that you may be rid of this dream of delusion forever.* Meditate deeply and faithfully, and one day you will wake up in ecstasy with God and see how foolish it is that people think they are suffering. You and I and they are all pure Spirit.

❖ ❖ ❖

Be not afraid of the frightening dream of this world. Awaken in God's immortal light! There was a time when life, to me, was like helplessly watching a terrifying movie, and I was giving too much importance to the tragedies being enacted therein. Then, one day while I was meditating, a great light appeared in my room and God's voice said to me: "What are you dreaming about? Behold My eternal light, in which the many nightmares of the world come and go. They are not real." What a tremendous consolation it was! Nightmares, however dreadful, are merely nightmares. Movies, whether enjoyable or disturbing, are merely movies. We ought not to keep our minds so absorbed in the sad and frightening dramas of this life. Is it not wiser to place our attention on that Power which is indestructible and unchanging? Why worry about the unpleasant surprises in the plot of this world movie! We are here for just a little while. Learn the lesson of the drama of life and find your freedom.

❖ ❖ ❖

* See *maya* in glossary.

Just beneath the shadows of this life is God's wondrous Light. The universe is a vast temple of His presence. When you meditate, you will find doors opening to Him everywhere. When you have communion with Him, not all the ravages of the world can take away that Joy and Peace.

Affirmation

In life and death, in disease, famine, pestilence, or poverty may I ever cling to Thee. Help me to realize I am immortal Spirit, untouched by the changes of childhood, youth, age, and world upheavals.

CHAPTER 5

Wisdom to Solve Problems and Make Life's Decisions

The world will go on like this in its ups and downs. Where shall we look for a sense of direction? Not to the prejudices roused within us by our habits and the environmental influences of our families, our country, or the world; but to the guiding voice of Truth within.

❖ ❖ ❖

Truth is no theory, no speculative system of philosophy. Truth is exact correspondence with Reality. For man, truth is unshakable knowledge of his real nature, his Self as soul.

❖ ❖ ❖

In everyday living, truth is a consciousness that is guided by spiritual wisdom, which propels us to do certain things, not because anybody says to, but because they are right.

❖ ❖ ❖

When you are in direct contact with the Creator of this universe, you are in direct contact with all wisdom and understanding.

❖ ❖ ❖

It is not a pumping-in from the outside that gives wisdom; it is the power and extent of your inner receptivity that determines how much you can attain of true knowledge, and how rapidly.

❖ ❖ ❖

When a problem comes up, instead of dwelling on it, think of every possible avenue of action to rid yourself of it. If you are unable to think, compare your particular trouble with others' similar troubles, and from their experiences learn which ways lead to failure and which ways lead to success. Choose those steps that seem logical and practical, and then get busy implementing them. The whole library of the universe is hidden within you. All the things you want to know are within yourself. To bring them out, think creatively.

❖ ❖ ❖

Perhaps you are seriously concerned about your child, or your health, or a mortgage payment. Not finding an immediate solution, you start worrying about the situation. And what do you get? A headache, nervousness, heart trouble. Because you do not clearly analyze yourself and your problems, you do not know how to control your feelings or the condition that confronts you. Instead of wasting time worrying, think positively about how the cause of the problem can be removed. If you want to get rid of a trouble, calmly analyze your difficulty, setting down point by point the pros and cons of the matter; then determine what steps might be best to accomplish your goal.

❖ ❖ ❖

There is always a way out of your trouble; and if you take the time to think clearly, to think how to get rid of the cause of your anxiety instead of just worrying about it, you become a master.

❖ ❖ ❖

All successful men and women devote much time to deep concentration. They are able to dive deeply within their minds and to find the pearls of right solutions for the problems that confront them. If you learn how to withdraw your attention from all objects of distraction and to place it upon one object of concentration,* you too will know how to attract at will whatever you need.

Developing Discriminative Judgment

When the mind is calm, how quickly, how smoothly, how beautifully you will perceive everything.

❖ ❖ ❖

A calm person reflects restfulness in his eyes, keen intelligence in his face, and proper receptivity in his mind. He is a man of decisive and prompt action, but he is not moved by impulses and desires that suddenly occur to him.

❖ ❖ ❖

Always think first of what you are about to do and how it will affect you. To act on impulse is not freedom, for you will be bound by the unpleasant effects of wrong actions. But to do those things your discrimination tells you are good for you is all-freeing. That kind of wisdom-guided action makes for a divine existence.

* A reference to the scientific yoga techniques of concentration taught in *Self-Realization Fellowship Lessons.*

❖ ❖ ❖

Man should not be a psychological automaton, like the animal, which acts only through instinct. To be unthinking is a great sin against Spirit, which abides in you; we are meant to be conscious of what we do. We should reflect before we act. We should learn how to use our minds so that we can evolve and realize our oneness with the Creator. Everything we do should be the result of premeditated thought.

❖ ❖ ❖

A student had made a serious error. She lamented, "I have always cultivated good habits. It seems incredible that this misfortune should have happened to me."

"Your mistake was to rely too heavily on good habits and to neglect constant exercise of right judgment," Paramahansa Yogananda said. "Your good habits help you in ordinary and familiar situations but may not suffice to guide you when a new problem arises. Then discrimination is necessary. By deeper meditation you will learn to choose the right course in everything, even when confronted by extraordinary circumstances.

"Man is not an automaton, and therefore cannot always live wisely by simply following set rules and rigid moral precepts. In the great variety of daily problems and events, we find scope for the development of good judgment."

❖ ❖ ❖

Good judgment is a natural expression of wisdom; but it is directly dependent on harmony within, which is poise of mind. When the mind lacks harmony, it has no peace; and without peace it lacks both judgment and wisdom. Life is full of bumps and knocks. In the hours of trials, which demand your keenest judgment, if you preserve your mental equilibrium you will attain victory. Inner harmony is your greatest supporter in bearing the burden of life.

❖ ❖ ❖

Restlessness—that which ruffles and diffuses the mind — blurs vision and causes misunderstanding. Emotion blurs your vision. Moods blur your vision. Most people act, not out of understanding, but according to their moods.

❖ ❖ ❖

Understanding is the vision of your inner being, the sight of your soul, the telescope of your heart. Understanding is a balance of calm intelligence and purity of heart....Emotion is distorted feeling that will lead you to do the wrong thing. And understanding that is guided solely by the intellect is coldblooded; it too will teach you to do wrong....You must have balanced understanding. If your understanding is governed by both heart and head, then you have clear vision to see yourself and others.

❖ ❖ ❖

You should analyze the many prejudices that your understanding is subject to. Any time you are making a decision or taking action, ask yourself if you are doing it through understanding, or through emotion or some other prejudicial influence on your mind. As long as you are subject to greed or anger; as long as you are influenced by the wrong thinking of others; as long as you are affected by the misunderstanding of others, so long will your own understanding be unclear.

❖ ❖ ❖

Human reason can always find the "pros and cons" for good and for bad actions alike; it is inherently disloyal. Discrimination acknowledges only one polestar criterion: the soul.

❖ ❖ ❖

Picture two men. On their right is the valley of life, and on their left is the valley of death. Both are men of reason, but one goes right and the other goes left. Why? Because one has used correctly his power of discrimination, and the other has misused that power by indulging in false rationalizations.

❖ ❖ ❖

Watch your motives in everything. Both the greedy man and the yogi eat. But would you say that eating is a sin because it is often associated with greed? No. Sin lies in the thought, in the motive. The worldly man eats to satisfy his greed, and the yogi eats to keep his body well. There is a lot of difference. Similarly, one man commits murder and is hanged for it; another man kills many human beings on the battlefield in defense of his country and is given a medal. Again, it is the motive that makes the difference. Moralists make absolute rules, but I am giving you illustrations to show you how you can live in this world of relativity with self-control of feeling but without being an automaton.

❖ ❖ ❖

The scientific way to live is to go within yourself and ask yourself whether you are doing right or wrong, and be absolutely sincere with yourself. If you are sincere with yourself, you are unlikely ever to go wrong; and even if you do, you will be able quickly to correct yourself.

❖ ❖ ❖

Every morning and night go into silence or deep meditation, for meditation is the only way to discriminate between truth and error.

❖ ❖ ❖

Learn to be guided by your conscience, the divine discriminative power within you.

❖ ❖ ❖

God is the whisper in the temple of your conscience, and He is the light of intuition. You know when you are doing wrong; your whole being tells you, and that feeling is God's voice. If you don't listen to Him, He becomes quiet. But when you wake up from your delusion, and want to do right, He will guide you.

❖ ❖ ❖

By constantly following the inner voice of conscience, which is the voice of God, you will become
a truly moral person, a highly spiritual being, a man
of peace.

Intuition: Insight of the Soul

Intuition is soul guidance, appearing naturally in
man during those instants when his mind is calm.
...The goal of yoga science is to calm the mind, that
without distortion it may hear the infallible counsel
of the Inner Voice.

❖ ❖ ❖

"Solve all your problems through meditation,"
[Lahiri Mahasaya said]. "Attune yourself to the active
inner Guidance; the Divine Voice has the answer to
every dilemma of life. Though man's ingenuity for
getting himself into trouble appears to be endless, the
Infinite Succor is no less resourceful."

❖ ❖ ❖

In wanting us to depend on Him alone, God does
not mean that you should not think for yourself; He
wants you to use your initiative. The idea is, if you
fail to seek conscious attunement with God first, you
cut off the Source, and so you cannot receive His help.
When you look to Him first for all things, He will
guide you; He will reveal to you what your mistakes
are so that you can change yourself and change the
course of your life.

❖ ❖ ❖

Remember, greater than a million reasonings of

the mind is to sit and meditate upon God until you feel calmness within. Then say to the Lord, "I can't solve my problem alone, even if I thought a zillion different thoughts; but I can solve it by placing it in Your hands, asking first for Your guidance, and then following through by thinking out the various angles for a possible solution." God does help those who help themselves. When your mind is calm and filled with faith after praying to God in meditation, you are able to see various answers to your problems; and because your mind is calm, you are capable of picking out the best solution. Follow that solution, and you will meet with success. This is applying the science of religion in your daily life.

❖ ❖ ❖

"Human life is beset with sorrow until we know how to tune in with the Divine Will, whose 'right course' is often baffling to the egoistic intelligence," [Sri Yukteswar said]. "God alone gives unerring counsel; who but He bears the burden of the cosmos?"

❖ ❖ ❖

When we know the Heavenly Father, we will have the answers not only to our own problems, but to those that beset the world. Why do we live, and why do we die? Why the present happenings, and why those of the past? I doubt there will ever come on earth any saint who will answer all the questions of all human beings. But in the temple of meditation every riddle of life that troubles our hearts shall be resolved. We will learn the answers to the puzzles of

life, and find the solution to all our difficulties, when
we come in contact with God.

Affirmation

*Heavenly Father, I will reason, I will will, I
will act; but guide Thou my reason, will, and
activity to the right thing that I should do.*

CHAPTER 6

Achieving Your Goals

Nothing is impossible, unless you think it is.

❖ ❖ ❖

As a mortal being you are limited, but as a child of God you are unlimited....Focus your attention on God, and you shall have all the power you want, to use in any direction.

Using Dynamic Will Power

Will is the instrument of the image of God within you. In will lies His limitless power, the power that controls all the forces of nature. As you are made in His image, that power is yours to bring about whatever you desire.

❖ ❖ ❖

When you make up your mind to do good things, you will accomplish them if you use dynamic will power to follow through. No matter what the circumstances are, if you go on trying, God will create the means by which your will shall find its proper reward. This is the truth Jesus referred to when he said: "If ye have faith, and doubt not,...if ye shall say unto this mountain, Be thou removed, and be thou cast into the sea, it shall be done."* If you continuously use your will power, no matter what reverses come, it

* Matthew 21:21.

will produce success and health and power to help
people, and above all, it will produce communion
with God.

❖ ❖ ❖

Once you have said, "I will," never give in. If you
say, "I will never catch cold," and the next morning you
have a terrible cold and are discouraged, you are allow-
ing your will to remain weak. You must not get discouraged when you see something happening that is
contrary to what you have affirmed. Keep on believing,
knowing it will be so. If outwardly you say, "I will," but
inwardly think, "I can't," then you neutralize the power
of thought and emasculate your will.

❖ ❖ ❖

If you want a home, and the mind says, "You sim-
pleton, you can't afford a house," you must make
your will stronger. When the "can't" disappears from
your mind, divine power comes. A home will not be
dropped down to you from heaven; you have to pour
forth will power continuously through constructive
actions. When you persist, refusing to accept failure,
the object of will must materialize. When you continuously work that will through your thoughts and
activities, what you are wishing for has to come
about. Even though there is nothing in the world to
conform to your wish, when your will persists, the
desired result will somehow manifest.

❖ ❖ ❖

Mortal man's brain is full of "can'ts." Being born
in a family with certain characteristics and habits, he

is influenced by these to think he can't do certain things; he can't walk much, he can't eat this, he can't stand that. Those "can'ts" have to be cauterized. You have within you the power to accomplish everything you want; that power lies in the will.

❖ ❖ ❖

If you cling to a certain thought with dynamic will power, it finally assumes a tangible outward form.

❖ ❖ ❖

Carrying a thought with dynamic will power means holding to it until that thought pattern develops dynamic force. When a thought is made dynamic by will force, it can manifest according to the mental blueprint you have created.

❖ ❖ ❖

How can you develop will? Choose some objective that you think you cannot accomplish, and then try with all your might to do that one thing. When you have achieved success, go on to something bigger and keep on exercising your will power in this way. If your difficulty is great, deeply pray: "Lord, give me the power to conquer all my difficulties." You must *use* your will power, no matter what you are, or who you are. *You must make up your mind.* Use this will power both in business and in meditation.

❖ ❖ ❖

If, after calmly reasoning, you make up your mind that what you have set out to do is right, then nobody should be able to stop you. If I had no job I would shake up the whole world until people would say, "Give him a job to keep him quiet!"

❖ ❖ ❖

If you have convinced yourself that you are a helpless mortal, and you allow everyone else to convince you that you can't get a job, then you have passed the decree in your own mind that you are down and done for. No judgment from God or fate, but your own pronouncement on yourself, keeps you poor or worried. Success or failure is determined in your own mind. Even against the negative opinion of the rest of society, if you bring out by your all-conquering God-given will the conviction that you cannot be left to suffer in difficulties, you will feel a secret divine power coming upon you; and you will see that the magnetism of that conviction and power is opening up new ways for you.

Dealing Constructively With Failure

The season of failure is the best time for sowing the seeds of success. The bludgeon of circumstances may bruise you, but keep your head erect. Always try *once more*, no matter how many times you have failed. Fight when you think that you can fight no longer, or when you think that you have already done your best, or until your efforts are crowned with success.

❖ ❖ ❖

Learn how to use the psychology of victory. Some people advise, "Don't talk about failure at all." But that alone won't help. First, analyze your failure and its causes, benefit from the experience, and then dismiss all thought of it. Though he fail many times, the man who keeps on striving, who is undefeated within, is a truly victorious person.

❖ ❖ ❖

Life may be dark, difficulties may come, opportunities may slip by unutilized, but never within yourself say, "I am done for. God has forsaken me." Who could do anything for that kind of person? Your family may forsake you; good fortune may seemingly desert you; all the forces of man and nature may be arrayed against you; but by the quality of divine initiative within you, you can defeat every invasion of fate created by your own past wrong actions, and march victorious into paradise.

❖ ❖ ❖

If you are guided by the Divine Consciousness, then even when the future seems absolutely black, everything ultimately will come out all right. When God guides you, you cannot fail.

❖ ❖ ❖

You must banish the thought that the Lord with His wonderful power is far away in heaven, and that you are a helpless little worm buried in difficulties down here on earth. Remember that behind your will is the great Divine Will.

❖ ❖ ❖

To stumble and fall into wrong ways is only momentary weakness. Do not think yourself wholly lost. The same ground on which you fall can be used as a support to help you get up again, if you learn from your experiences.

❖ ❖ ❖

If you recognize a mistake and resolutely determine not to make it again, then even if you fall, that fall will be very much less than if you had never tried.

❖ ❖ ❖

Nor should we expect to be successful in all our attempts. Some ventures may fail, but others will be successful. Success and failure are interrelated; one cannot exist without the other.... So we should not become egotistical and overpowered with pride if we find abundant success; nor should we lose heart and become discouraged if we meet with failure.

❖ ❖ ❖

No matter how many times you fail, keep on trying. No matter what happens, if you have unalterably resolved, "The earth may be shattered, but I will keep on doing the best I can," you are using dynamic will, and you will succeed. That dynamic will is what makes one man rich and another man strong and another man a saint.

❖ ❖ ❖

Concentration: A Key to Success

The root cause of many failures in life is lack of concentration. Attention is like a searchlight; when its beam is spread over a vast area, its power to focus on a particular object becomes weak, but focused on one thing at a time, it becomes powerful. Great men are men of concentration. They put their whole mind on one thing at a time.

❖ ❖ ❖

One should know the scientific method of concentration* by which he may disengage his attention from objects of distraction and focus it upon one thing at a time. By the power of concentration, man can use the untold power of mind to accomplish that which he desires, and he can guard all doors through which failure may enter.

❖ ❖ ❖

Many persons think that their actions have to be either restless or slow. That is not true. If you keep calm, with intense concentration, you will perform all duties with the correct speed.

❖ ❖ ❖

A calm person has his senses fully identified with the environment in which he places himself. A restless person does not notice anything; consequently he gets into trouble with himself and others and misunderstands everything.... Never change the center of

* Taught in *Self-Realization Fellowship Lessons.*

your concentration from calmness to restlessness. Perform activities only with concentration.

❖ ❖ ❖

Always center your whole mind on whatever you may be doing, however small or seemingly unimportant it may be. Also learn to keep your mind flexible so that you can transfer your attention at a moment's notice. But above all do everything with one hundred percent concentration.

❖ ❖ ❖

Most people do everything half-heartedly. They use only about one-tenth of their attention. That is why they haven't the power to succeed....[Do] everything with the power of attention. The full force of that power can be attained through meditation. When you use that focusing power of God, you can place it on anything and be a success.

Creativity

Tune yourself with the creative power of Spirit. You will be in contact with the Infinite Intelligence that is able to guide you and to solve all problems. Power from the dynamic Source of your being will flow uninterruptedly so that you will be able to perform creatively in any sphere of activity.

❖ ❖ ❖

Ask yourself this question: "Have I ever tried to do anything that nobody else has done?" That is the starting point in the application of initiative. If you haven't thought that far, you are like hundreds of others who erroneously think they have no power to act differently than they do. They are like sleepwalkers; the suggestions coming from their subconscious mind have given them the consciousness of one-horsepower people.

If you have been going through life in this somnambulistic state, you must wake yourself by affirming: "I have man's greatest quality — initiative. Every human being has some spark of power by which he can create something that has not been created before. Yet I see how easily I could be deluded with the mortal consciousness of limitation that pervades the world, if I allowed myself to be hypnotized by environment!"

❖ ❖ ❖

What is initiative? It is a creative faculty within you, a spark of the Infinite Creator. It may give you the power to create something no one else has ever created. It urges you to do things in new ways. The accomplishments of a person of initiative may be as spectacular as a shooting star. Apparently creating something from nothing, he demonstrates that the seemingly impossible may become possible by one's employment of the great inventive power of the Spirit.

❖ ❖ ❖

The one who creates does not wait for an opportunity, blaming circumstances, the fates, and the gods. He seizes opportunities or creates them with the magic wand of his will, effort, and searching discrimination.

❖ ❖ ❖

Before embarking on important undertakings, sit quietly, calm your senses and thoughts, and meditate deeply. You will then be guided by the great creative power of Spirit.

❖ ❖ ❖

Whatever you want to do, think about it until you are lost in that idea. Think, think, think, and make plans. Then take a little time; don't jump into anything at once. Take a step, and then think more. Something within tells you what to do. Do it, and think some more. Some further guidance will come. By learning to go deep within, you will connect your consciousness with the superconsciousness of the soul, so that with infinite will power, patience, and intuition you can grow those idea-seeds of success.

❖ ❖ ❖

As soon as you think a right thought, work it. Some people have a good idea but they haven't the tenacity to think it through and work it out. You must have courage and perseverance, and think, "I am going to see my idea through. It may be that I won't win out in this life, but I will make the effort." Think and act, think and act. That is how to develop your mind power. Every idea is a little seed, but you have to grow it.

❖ ❖ ❖

Many people try to achieve something in the realm of thought, but they give up when difficulties arise. Only those persons who have visualized their thoughts very strongly have been able to manifest them in outward form.

❖ ❖ ❖

Imagination [the power to image or visualize] is a very important factor in creative thought. But imagination has to be ripened into conviction. You can't do that without a strong will. But if you imagine something with all the power of your will, your imagination will be converted into conviction. And when you can hold that conviction against all odds, it will come true.

❖ ❖ ❖

Make mental blueprints of little things, and keep on making them materialize until you can make your big dreams also come true.

❖ ❖ ❖

Men of success are those who have forethought enough to make an indelible blueprint in their minds of whatever they wish to build or produce upon this earth. Backed by the financier of their creative ability, they employ their will power as contractor, their detailed attention as carpenters, and their mental patience as the necessary labor to materialize in true life the desired result or object.

❖ ❖ ❖

Whenever you want to produce something, do not depend upon the outside source; go deep and seek the Infinite Source. All methods of business success, all inventions, all vibrations of music, and all inspirational thoughts and writings are recorded in the annals of God.

❖ ❖ ❖

Work on your progress with God. This is the most important of all creative thinking.

Creating All-Round Success

He is wisest who seeks God. He is the most successful who has found God.

❖ ❖ ❖

Success is not a simple matter; it cannot be determined merely by the amount of money and material possessions you have. The meaning of success goes far deeper. It can only be measured by the extent to which your inner peace and mental control enable you to be happy under all circumstances. That is real success.

❖ ❖ ❖

Great teachers will never counsel you to be neglectful; they will teach you to be balanced. You have to work, no doubt, to feed and clothe the body. But if you allow one duty to contradict another, it is not a true duty. Thousands of businessmen are so busy gathering wealth, they forget that they are creating a lot of heart disease too! If duty to prosperity makes you forget duty to health, it is not duty. One should develop in a harmonious way. There is no use giving special attention to developing a wonderful body, if it houses a peanut brain. The mind also must be developed. And if you have excellent health and prosperity and intellect, but you are not happy, then you have still not made a success of your life. When you can truthfully say, "I am happy, and no one can take my happiness away from me," you are a king—you have found the image of God within you.

❖ ❖ ❖

Another qualification of success is that we not only bring harmonious and beneficial results to ourselves, but also share those benefits with others.

❖ ❖ ❖

Life should be chiefly service. Without that ideal, the intelligence that God has given you is not reaching out toward its goal. When in service you forget the little self, you will feel the big Self of Spirit. As the vital rays of the sun nurture all, so should you spread rays of hope in the hearts of the poor and forsaken, kindle courage in the hearts of the despondent, and light a new strength in the hearts of those who think that they are failures. When you realize that life is a joyous battle of duty and at the same time a passing dream, and when you become filled with the joy of making others happy by giving them kindness and peace, in God's eyes your life is a success.

❖ ❖ ❖

The Value of Enthusiasm

Work of any kind, if done in the right spirit, gives you victory over yourself....The attitude with which you work is what counts. Mental laziness and working unwillingly spoil one. People often ask me, "How do you do so many things?" It is because I do everything with the greatest pleasure and spirit of service. Inwardly I am all the time with God. And though I sleep very little I always feel fresh, because I perform my duties with the right attitude: that it is a privilege to serve.

❖ ❖ ❖

Mental unwillingness to work is accompanied by listlessness and lack of energy. Enthusiasm and willingness go hand in hand with fresh supplies of energy. From these facts we can see the subtle relationship between will and energy. The greater the will, the more inexhaustible the energy.

❖ ❖ ❖

If your work in life is humble, do not apologize for it. Be proud because you are fulfilling the duty given you by the Father. He needs you in your particular place; all people cannot play the same role. So long as you work to please God, all cosmic forces will harmoniously assist you.

❖ ❖ ❖

In God's eyes nothing is large or small. Were it not for His perfect nicety in constructing the tiny atom, could the skies wear the proud structures of

Vega, Arcturus? Distinctions of "important" and "unimportant" are surely unknown to the Lord, lest, for want of a pin, the cosmos collapse!

❖ ❖ ❖

Try to do little things in an extraordinary way.

❖ ❖ ❖

You should progress — try to be the very best in your profession. Express the limitless power of soul in anything you take up....You must constantly create and produce new successes and not become [an] automaton. All work is purifying if done with the right motive.

❖ ❖ ❖

We should approach our nearest problem or duty with concentrated energy and execute it to perfection. This should be our philosophy of life.

❖ ❖ ❖

By stick-to-itiveness, by cultivating creative originality and developing your talents through the unlimited power of God that comes from communion with Him daily in deep meditation; by honest business methods, loyalty to your employer, and thinking of his business as if it were your own; and by cultivating an intuitive attunement with your immediate superior or with the owner of the business and with your Cosmic Employer—God—you may unfailingly please your employer in the office and your Divine Employer.

❖ ❖ ❖

It is easy to be idle or filled with hopelessness and thus desist from striving for financial success in life. It is easy to earn money dishonestly when such opportunity presents itself. But it is wrong thus to excuse oneself from making an effort to sustain himself honorably....

It is an exceptional man who earns money abundantly, unselfishly, honestly, quickly, just for God and His work and for making others happy. Such activity develops many sterling qualities of character that aid one on the spiritual path as well as the material path. Making money honestly and industriously to serve God's work is the next greatest art after the art of realizing God. Responsibility, knowledge of organization, order, leadership, and practical usefulness are developed in creating business success and are necessary for the all-round growth of man.

Abundance and Prosperity

Those who seek prosperity for themselves alone are in the end bound to become poor, or to suffer from mental inharmony; but those who consider the whole world as their home, and who really care and work for group or world prosperity... find the individual prosperity that is legitimately theirs. This is a sure and secret law.

❖ ❖ ❖

Unselfishness is the governing principle in the law of prosperity.

❖ ❖ ❖

I own nothing, yet I know that if I were hungry there would be thousands in the world who would feed me, because I have given to thousands. That same law will work for whoever thinks not of himself as the one who is going to starve, but of the other person in need.

❖ ❖ ❖

Every day, do some good to help others, even if it is only a pittance. If you want to love God you must love people. They are His children. You can be helpful materially by giving to the needy; and mentally by giving comfort to the sorrowful, courage to the fearful, divine friendship and moral support to the weak. You also sow seeds of goodness when you interest others in God, and cultivate in them greater love for God, deeper faith in Him. When you leave this world, material riches will be left behind; but every good that you have done will go with you. Wealthy people who live in miserliness, and selfish people who never help others, do not attract wealth in their next life. But those who give and share, whether they have much or little, will attract prosperity. That is the law of God.

❖ ❖ ❖

Think of Divine Abundance as a mighty, refreshing rain; whatever receptacle you have at hand will receive it. If you hold up a tin cup, you will receive only that quantity. If you hold up a bowl, that will be filled. What kind of receptacle are you holding up to Divine Abundance? Perhaps your vessel is defective;

if so, it should be repaired by casting out all fear, hate, doubt, and envy, and then cleansed by the purifying waters of peace, tranquility, devotion, and love. Divine Abundance follows the law of service and generosity. Give and then receive. Give to the world the best you have and the best will come back to you.

❖ ❖ ❖

Thanksgiving and praise open in your consciousness the way for spiritual growth and supply to come to you. Spirit pushes Itself out into visible manifestation as soon as a channel is opened through which It can flow.

❖ ❖ ❖

"To men who meditate on Me as their Very Own, ever united to Me by incessant worship, I supply their deficiencies and make permanent their gains."* [Those] who are faithful to their Creator, perceiving Him in all the diverse phases of life, discover that He has taken charge of their lives even in the smallest detail, and with divine foresight makes smooth their paths....

This stanza of the Gita reminds us of Christ's words: "But seek ye first the kingdom of God, and His righteousness; and all these things shall be added unto you."†

❖ ❖ ❖

* Bhagavad Gita IX:22.
† Matthew 6:33.

Affirmations for Success

I will go forth in perfect faith in the power of Omnipresent Good to bring me what I need at the time I need it.

❖ ❖ ❖

Within me is the Infinite Creative Power. I shall not go to the grave without some accomplishments. I am a God-man, a rational creature. I am the power of Spirit, the dynamic Source of my soul. I shall create revelations in the world of business, in the world of thought, in the world of wisdom. I and my Father are One. I can create anything I desire, even as my creative Father.

Affirmations for Divine Abundance

O Father, I want prosperity, health, and wisdom without measure, not from earthly sources but from Thine all-possessing, all-powerful, all-bountiful hands.

I will not be a beggar, asking limited mortal prosperity, health, and knowledge. I am Thy child, and as such I demand, without limitations, a divine son's share of Thine illimitable riches.

❖ ❖ ❖

Divine Father, this is my prayer: I care not what I permanently possess, but give me power to acquire at will whatever I daily need.

CHAPTER 7

Inner Peace: Antidote for Stress, Worry, and Fear

Calmness is the ideal state in which we should receive all life's experiences. Nervousness is the opposite of calmness, and its prevalence today makes it very nearly a world disease.

❖ ❖ ❖

Only those who partake of the harmony within their souls know the harmony that runs through nature. Whosoever lacks this inner harmony feels also a lack of it in the world. The mind in chaos finds chaos all around. How can one know what peace is like if he has never tasted it? But he who has inner peace can abide in this state even in the midst of outer discord.

❖ ❖ ❖

When you worry, there is static coming through your mind radio. God's song is the song of calmness. Nervousness is the static; calmness is the voice of God speaking to you through the radio of your soul.

❖ ❖ ❖

Calmness is the living breath of God's immortality in you.

❖ ❖ ❖

Everything you do should be done with peace. That is the best medicine for your body, mind, and soul. It is the most wonderful way to live.

❖ ❖ ❖

Peace is the altar of God, the condition in which happiness exists.

❖ ❖ ❖

If you keep your mind on the resolve never to lose your peace, then you can attain godliness. Keep a secret chamber of silence within yourself, where you will not let moods, trials, battles, or inharmony enter. Keep out all hatred, revengefulness, and desires. In this chamber of peace God will visit you.

❖ ❖ ❖

You cannot buy peace; you must know how to manufacture it within, in the stillness of your daily practices in meditation.

❖ ❖ ❖

We should pattern our life by a triangular guide: calmness and sweetness are the two sides; the base is happiness. Every day, one should remind himself: "I am a prince of peace, sitting on the throne of poise, directing my kingdom of activity." Whether one acts quickly or slowly, in solitude or in the busy marts of men, his center should be peaceful, poised.

Nervousness

One who is naturally calm does not lose his sense of reason, justice, or humor under any circumstances. . . . He does not poison his bodily tissues with anger or fear, which adversely affect circulation. It is a well-proven fact that the milk of an angry mother can have a harmful effect on her child. What more striking proof can we ask for, that violent emotions will finally reduce the body to an ignominious wreck?

❖ ❖ ❖

Indulgence in constant thoughts of fear, anger, melancholy, remorse, envy, sorrow, hatred, discontent, or worry; and lack of the necessities for normal and happy living, such as right food, proper exercise, fresh air, sunshine, agreeable work and a purpose in life, all are causes of nervous disease.

❖ ❖ ❖

If we connect a 120-volt bulb with a 2,000-volt source, it would burn out the bulb. Similarly, the nervous system was not made to withstand the destructive force of intense emotion or persistent negative thoughts and feelings.

❖ ❖ ❖

But nervousness can be cured. The sufferer must be willing to analyze his condition and remove the disintegrating emotions and negative thoughts that are little by little destroying him. Objective analysis of one's problems,* and maintaining calmness in all situations of life will heal the most persistent case of nervousness....The victim of nervousness must understand his case, and must reflect on those continual mistakes of thinking which are responsible for his maladjustment to life.

* See chapter 5.

❖ ❖ ❖

Instead of hurrying in a state of emotional excitement to get some place, and then not enjoying it once you arrive because you are restless, try to be more calm....As soon as your mind becomes restless, give it a whack with your will and order it to be calm.

❖ ❖ ❖

Excitement upsets the nervous balance, sending too much energy to some parts and depriving others of their normal share. This lack of proper distribution of nerve force is the sole cause of nervousness.

❖ ❖ ❖

A body that is relaxed and calm invites mental peace.

❖ ❖ ❖

[Technique* for relaxing the body:]

Tense with will: By command of will, direct the life energy (through the process of tension) to flood the body or any body part. Feel the energy vibrating there, energizing and revitalizing. *Relax and feel:* Relax the tension, and feel the soothing tingle of new life and vitality in the recharged area. *Feel* that you are not the body; you are that life which sustains the

* Simplified reference to a special technique developed in 1916 by Paramahansa Yogananda to recharge the body with vitality and to promote perfect relaxation; taught in *Self-Realization Fellowship Lessons.* The general principle of tensing and relaxing has in recent years been popularly endorsed and used by medical science as an aid in many maladies, including reduction of nervousness and high blood pressure.

body. *Feel* the peace, the freedom, the increased awareness that comes with the calmness produced by the
practice of this technique.

❖ ❖ ❖

When you have peace in every movement of your
body, and peace in your thinking, and in your will
power, and peace in your love, and peace and God in
your ambitions, remember—you have connected God
with your life.

Worry and Fear

Although life seems capricious, uncertain, and
full of all kinds of troubles, still we are always under
the guiding, loving protection of God.

❖ ❖ ❖

Don't make a fuss about anything. Whenever you
worry, remember, you are deepening the cosmic delusion within you.*

❖ ❖ ❖

Fear of failure or sickness is cultivated by turning
over such thoughts in the conscious mind until they
become rooted in the subconscious and finally in the
superconscious.† Then the superconsciously and sub-
consciously rooted fear begins to germinate and fill

---

* Man's forgetfulness of his true omnipotent soul nature, and of its
divine connection with God, is the cause of all his suffering and
limitation. Yoga teaches that this oblivion or ignorance is caused by
maya, or cosmic delusion.

† The higher mind from which the subconscious and conscious
minds derive their power.

the conscious mind with fear plants that are not so easy to destroy as the original thought would have been, and these eventually bear their poisonous, death-dealing fruits....

Uproot them from within by forceful concentration upon courage, and by shifting your consciousness to the absolute peace of God within.

❖ ❖ ❖

Whatever it is that you fear, take your mind away from it and leave it to God. Have faith in Him. Much suffering is due simply to worry. Why suffer now when the malady has not yet come? Since most of our ills come through fear, if you give up fear you will be free at once. The healing will be instant. Every night, before you sleep, affirm: "The Heavenly Father is with me; I am protected." Mentally surround yourself with Spirit....You will feel His wonderful protection.

❖ ❖ ❖

When the consciousness is kept on God, you will have no fears; every obstacle will then be overcome by courage and faith.

❖ ❖ ❖

Fear comes from the heart. If ever you feel overcome by dread of some illness or accident, you should inhale and exhale deeply, slowly, and rhythmically several times, relaxing with each exhalation. This helps the circulation to become normal. If your heart is truly quiet you cannot feel fear at all.

❖ ❖ ❖

The trouble with us is that instead of living only in the present, we try to live in the past and in the future at the same time. These loads are too heavy for the mind to carry, so we must restrict the amount of the load. The past is gone. Why continue to carry it in the mind? Let the mind take care of its burdens one at a time. A swan eats only the solid content from the liquid he scoops up in his bill; similarly, we should keep in mind only the lessons we have learned from the past and forget unnecessary details. This will relieve the mind to a great extent.

❖ ❖ ❖

When we have too much to do at one time, we become very discouraged. Instead of worrying about what should be done, just say: "This hour is mine. I will do the best I can." The clock cannot tick twenty-four hours away in one minute, and you cannot do in one hour what you can do in twenty-four hours. Live each present moment completely and the future will take care of itself. Fully enjoy the wonder and beauty of each instant. Practice the presence of peace. The more you do that, the more you will feel the presence of that power in your life.

❖ ❖ ❖

The pleasure of modern man is in getting more and more, and what happens to anyone else doesn't matter. But isn't it better to live simply—without so many luxuries and with fewer worries? There is no pleasure in driving yourself until you cannot enjoy what you have....The time will come when mankind will begin to get away from the consciousness of needing so many material things. More security and peace will be found in the simple life.

❖ ❖ ❖

If you continually write out checks without depositing anything in your bank account, you will run out of money. So it is with your life. Without regular deposits of peace in your life account, you will run out of strength, calmness, and happiness. You will finally become bankrupt — emotionally, mentally, physically, and spiritually. But daily communion with God will continually replenish your inner bankroll.

❖ ❖ ❖

No matter how busy we are, we should not forget now and then to free our minds completely from worries and all duties....Try to remain for one minute at a time without thinking negatively, fixing the mind on the peace within, especially if worried. Then try to remain for several minutes with a quiet mind. Following that, think of some happy incident; dwell on it and visualize it; mentally go through some pleasant experience over and over again until you have forgotten your worries entirely.

❖ ❖ ❖

When beset by overwhelming mental trials or worries one should try to fall asleep. If he can do that, he will find upon awakening that the mental tension has been relieved, and that the worry has loosened its grip.* We need to remind ourselves at such times that even if we died, the earth would continue to follow its orbit, and business would be carried on as usual; so why worry?

❖ ❖ ❖

Life is entertaining when we do not take it too seriously. A good laugh is an excellent remedy for human ills. One of the best characteristics of the American people is their ability to laugh. To be able to laugh at life is marvelous. This my master [Swami Sri Yukteswar] taught me. In the beginning of my training in his hermitage, I went about with a solemn face, never smiling. One day Master pointedly remarked, "What is this? Are you attending a funeral ceremony? Don't you know that finding God is the funeral of all sorrows? Then why so glum? Don't take this life too seriously."

❖ ❖ ❖

Knowing that you are a child of God, make up your mind to be calm no matter what happens. If your mind is fully identified with your activities, you cannot be conscious of the Lord, but if you are calm and receptive to Him within while being active without, you are rightly active.

❖ ❖ ❖

Quiet the outgoing mental restlessness and turn

---

* As explained on pages 16–17, by going into the subconscious state of sleep the soul temporarily rises above troubles associated with attachment to the body and its experiences. An even greater method is to enter the superconscious state of communion with God through deep meditation.

the mind within. Harmonize your thoughts and desires with the all-fulfilling realities you already possess in your soul. Then you will see the underlying harmony in your life and in all nature. If you harmonize your hopes and expectations with this inherent harmony, you will float through life on buoyant wings of peace. The beauty and depth of Yoga lies in its bestowal of this invariable tranquility.*

❖ ❖ ❖

Realization that all power to think, speak, feel, and act comes from God, and that He is ever with us, inspiring and guiding us, brings an instant freedom from nervousness. Flashes of divine joy will come with this realization; sometimes a deep illumination will pervade one's being, banishing the very concept of fear. Like an ocean, the power of God sweeps in, surging through the heart in a cleansing flood, removing all obstructions of delusive doubt, nervousness, and fear. The delusion of matter, the consciousness of being only a mortal body, is overcome by contacting the sweet serenity of Spirit, attainable by daily med-

---

* "The state of complete mental tranquility, attained by yoga meditation, in which the self (ego) is satisfied by the vision of the Self (soul);

"The state in which the sense-transcendent bliss becomes known to the awakened intuitive intelligence, and in which the yogi remains enthroned, never again to be removed;

"The state that, once found, the yogi considers as the treasure beyond all other treasures — the state in which he is immune to even the mightiest grief;

"That state is known as Yoga — the pain-free state. The practice of Yoga is therefore to be observed resolutely and with a stout heart" (Bhagavad Gita VI:20–23).

itation. Then you know that the body is a little bubble of energy in His cosmic sea.

Affirmations for Peace and Calmness

I am a prince of peace, sitting on the throne of poise, directing the kingdom of activity.

❖ ❖ ❖

The moment I am restless or disturbed in mind, I will retire to silence and meditation until calmness is restored.

❖ ❖ ❖

I will be neither lazy nor feverishly active. In every challenge of life I shall do my best without worrying about the future.

CHAPTER 8

Bringing Out the Best Within You

We are what we *think* we are. The habitual inclination of our thoughts determines our talents and
abilities, and our personality. Thus, some *think* they
are writers or artists, industrious or lazy, and so on.
What if you want to be other than what you presently
think you are? You may argue that others have been
born with the special talent you lack but desire to
have. This is true. But they had to cultivate the habit
of that ability some time—if not in this life, then in
a previous one.* So whatever you want to be, start to
develop that pattern now. You can instill any trend in
your consciousness right now, provided you inject a
strong thought in your mind; then your actions and
whole being will obey that thought.

❖ ❖ ❖

One must never give up hope of becoming better.
A person is old only when he refuses to make the effort to change. That stagnant state is the only "old
age" I recognize. When a person says again and again,
"I can't change; this is the way I am," then I have to
say, "All right, stay that way, since you have made up
your mind to be like that."

❖ ❖ ❖

* See *reincarnation* in glossary.

85

No matter what his present state, man can change for the better through self-control, discipline, and following proper diet and health laws. Why do you think you cannot change? Mental laziness is the secret cause of all weakness.

❖ ❖ ❖

Everyone has self-limiting idiosyncrasies. These were not put into your nature by God, but were created by you. These are what you must change — by remembering that these habits, peculiar to your nature, are nothing but manifestations of your own thoughts.

❖ ❖ ❖

In the ultimate sense, all things are made of pure consciousness; their finite appearance is the result of the relativity of consciousness.* Therefore, if you want to change anything in yourself, you must change the process of thought that occasions the materialization of consciousness into different forms of matter and action. That is the way, the only way, to remold your life.

---

* Yoga teaches that the thought of God is the fundamental structure of creation. Just as steam becomes water by condensation, and by further condensation becomes ice, all patterns and forms of energy and matter are condensations of consciousness. Pioneering physicists of the twentieth century are rediscovering what the yogis have known since ancient times. Sir James Jeans, British scientist, wrote: "The universe begins to look more like a great thought than like a great machine." And Einstein said: "I want to know how God created this world. I am not interested in this or that phenomenon, in the spectrum of this or that element. I want to know His thoughts; the rest are details."

❖ ❖ ❖

Fortunately, we can start practicing any time and any place, concentrating upon developing those good qualities in which we are defective. If we are lacking in will power, let us concentrate upon that, and through conscious effort we shall be able to create strong will power in ourselves. If we want to relieve ourselves of fear, we should meditate upon courage, and in due time we shall be freed from the bondage of fear.

❖ ❖ ❖

Very simply, all you have to do is to think away the thoughts you want to destroy, by replacing them with constructive thoughts. This is the key to heaven; it is in your hands.

Introspection: A Secret of Progress

The first thing to do is to introspect. Take stock of yourself and your habits, and find out what is standing in your way. Often it is inertia, or lack of definite, undivided effort and attention. Sometimes there are habits that need to be weeded out of the garden of your life, so that true happiness may become more firmly rooted.

❖ ❖ ❖

One secret of progress is self-analysis. Introspection is a mirror in which to see recesses of your mind that otherwise would remain hidden from you. Diagnose your failures and sort out your good and bad tendencies. Analyze what you are, what you wish to become, and what shortcomings are impeding you.

❖ ❖ ❖

Millions of people never analyze themselves. Mentally they are mechanical products of the factory of their environment, preoccupied with breakfast, lunch, and dinner, working and sleeping, and going here and there to be entertained. They don't know what or why they are seeking, nor why they never realize complete happiness and lasting satisfaction. By evading self-analysis, people go on being robots, conditioned by their environment. True self-analysis is the greatest art of progress.

Everyone should learn to analyze himself dispassionately. Write down your thoughts and aspirations daily. Find out what you are—not what you imagine you are!—because you want to make yourself what you ought to be. Most people don't change because they don't see their own faults.

❖ ❖ ❖

One who has not kept a mental diary should begin this salutary practice. The knowledge of just how much and in what way he fails in the daily experiences of life may stimulate him to more effort to be what he should be. By keeping such a journal and by using discrimination to destroy the bad habits that create pain and suffering for ourselves and others, we will get rid of them. Every night we should ask ourselves: "How long have I been with God today?" We should analyze also how much we have deeply thought, how much we have accomplished in our duties, how much we have done for others, how we have governed ourselves in the various situations of the day.

❖ ❖ ❖

By watching the graphs of your mind, you can see whether you are progressing every day. You don't want to hide from yourself. You must know yourself as you are. By keeping a diary of your introspection, you keep watch on your bad habits and are better prepared to destroy them.

Conquering Temptations

Sometimes it seems difficult to be good, while it is easy to be bad; and that to give up the bad things is to miss something. But I say you will not miss anything but sorrow.

❖ ❖ ❖

Everything that the great ones have warned against is like poisoned honey. I say don't taste it. You may argue, "But it is sweet." Well, my reasoning is that after you have tasted the sweetness it will destroy you. Evil was made sweet to delude you. You have to use your discrimination to distinguish between poisoned honey and that which is in your best interest. Avoid those things that will ultimately hurt you, and choose those that will give you freedom and happiness.

❖ ❖ ❖

Sorrow, illness, and failure are natural results of transgressions against God's laws. Wisdom consists in avoiding such violations and finding peace and happiness within yourself through thoughts and actions that are in harmony with your real Self.

❖ ❖ ❖

Whenever there is an overwhelming desire in your heart...use your discrimination. Ask yourself, "Is it a good desire or a bad desire for which I seek fulfillment?"

❖ ❖ ❖

Material desires encourage our bad habits by engendering false hopes of satisfaction and happiness. At such times one should summon his discriminative powers to reveal the truth: Bad habits lead ultimately to unhappiness. Thus exposed, bad habits become impotent to hold man in their misery-making sway.

❖ ❖ ❖

Resisting temptations isn't the denial of all the pleasures of life; it is to have supernal control over what you want to do. I am showing you the way to real freedom, not the false sense of freedom that in fact is compelling you to do what your habits lead you to do.

❖ ❖ ❖

The old orthodox way is to deny temptation, to suppress it. But you must learn to *control* that temptation. It is not a sin to be tempted. Even though you are boiling with temptation, you are not evil; but if you yield to that temptation, you are caught temporarily by the power of evil. You must erect about yourself protecting parapets of wisdom. There is no stronger force that you can employ against temptation than wisdom. Complete understanding will bring you to the point where nothing can tempt you to actions that promise pleasure but in the end will only hurt you.

❖ ❖ ❖

Until you have attained wisdom, when temptation comes you must first stop the action or urge, and *then* reason. If you try to reason first, you will be compelled in spite of yourself to do the thing that you don't want to do, because temptation will overcome all reason. Just say "No!" and get up and go away. That is the surest way to escape the Devil.* The more you develop this "won't" power during the intrusion of temptation, the happier you will be; for all joy depends on the ability to do that which conscience tells you you *should* do.

❖ ❖ ❖

When you say *no* to temptation, you must mean *no*. Don't give in. The spineless weakling all the time says *yes*. But great minds are full of *no*s.

❖ ❖ ❖

* Satan; the conscious force of delusion that attempts to keep man in ignorance of his divine nature. See *maya* in glossary.

When you have made up your mind not to smoke, or eat unwisely, or lie or cheat, be firm in these good desires; don't weaken. Wrong environment saps your will and invites wrong desires. Live with thieves and you think that is the only life. But live with divine persons, and after having divine communion, no other desires can tempt you.

❖ ❖ ❖

If you have a particular bad habit or karmic inclination, don't mix with those who have the same kind of bad habit. If you tend to be greedy, avoid the company of others who are greedy. If you have a desire to drink, stay away from those who drink. People who support your bad habits are not your friends. They will cause you to throw away your soul's joy. Avoid the company of wrongdoers and mix with those who are good.

❖ ❖ ❖

The greatest influence in your life, stronger even than your will power, is your environment. Change that, if necessary.

❖ ❖ ❖

There are two kinds of environment that you should watch carefully—the outer and the inner.

❖ ❖ ❖

Watch your thoughts. All your experiences come percolating through your thoughts. It is the company of your thoughts that uplifts or degrades you.

❖ ❖ ❖

You must be stronger than the thoughts and suggestions constantly vibrating from other people. That is the way to conquer wrong vibrations that come into your environment.

❖ ❖ ❖

Think of God as your environment. Be one with God and nothing can harm you.

❖ ❖ ❖

Every action has a mental counterpart. We perform acts with our physical power, but that activity has its origin in the mind, and is guided by the mental captain. To steal is evil; but the greater evil is the mental act of stealing that initiates the physical theft, because mind is the real perpetrator. Whatever wrong action you want to avoid, first throw it out of the mind. If you concentrate only on the physical action, it is very hard to gain control. Concentrate on the mind: correct your thoughts, and automatically the actions will be taken care of.

❖ ❖ ❖

Every time a bad thought comes, cast it out. Then Satan can't do anything to you. But as soon as you think wrongly, you go toward Satan. You are constantly moving back and forth between good and evil; to escape, you must go where Satan will be unable to reach you: deep in the heart of God.

❖ ❖ ❖

Virtue and purity are not rooted in weakness. Rather, they are strong qualities that fight the forces of evil. It is within your power to choose how much purity, love, beauty, and spiritual joy you will express, not only through deeds, but in your thoughts, feelings, and desires....Keep a pure mind and you will find the Lord ever with you. You will hear Him talking to you in the language of your heart; you will glimpse Him in every flower and shrub, in every blade of grass, in every passing thought. "Blessed are the pure in heart: for they shall see God."*

❖ ❖ ❖

The best way to overcome temptation is by comparison. Meditate more and see if meditation doesn't give you more happiness.

❖ ❖ ❖

When you withdraw your mind inward [in meditation], you will begin to perceive that there are many more wonderful things within than outside.

❖ ❖ ❖

If you but *looked* at your soul, the all-perfect reflection of God within you, you would find all your desires satisfied!

❖ ❖ ❖

In the absence of inward joy, men turn to evil. Meditation on the God of Bliss permeates us with goodness.

* Matthew 5:8.

❖ ❖ ❖

The ego attempts to satisfy through material channels the soul's constant, insatiable longing for God. Far from accomplishing its objective, it increases man's misery. The soul's hunger can never be appeased by indulgence of the senses. When man realizes this and masters his ego, that is, when he achieves self-control, his life becomes glorified by the awareness of divine bliss while he is still in the flesh. Then, instead of being the slave of material desires and appetites, man's attention is transferred to the heart of Omnipresence, resting there forever with the hidden Joy in everything.

The Correct Attitude Toward Past Wrongs

Avoid dwelling on all the wrong things you have done. They do not belong to you now. Let them be forgotten. It is attention that creates habit and memory. As soon as you put the needle on a phonograph record, it begins to play. Attention is the needle that plays the record of past actions. So you should not put your attention on bad ones. Why go on suffering over the unwise actions of your past? Cast their memory from your mind, and take care not to repeat those actions again.

❖ ❖ ❖

You may be worried about the wrong you have committed, but God is not. What is past is past. You are His child, and whatever wrong you have done came about because you didn't know Him. He doesn't hold against you the evil done under the influence of ignorance. All He asks is that you not repeat your wrong actions. He wants only to find out whether or not you are sincere in your intention to be good.

❖ ❖ ❖

"Forget the past," [Sri Yukteswar said]. "The vanished lives of all men are dark with many shames. Human conduct is ever unreliable until man is anchored in the Divine. Everything in future will improve if you are making a spiritual effort now."

❖ ❖ ❖

Don't think of yourself as a sinner. You are a child of the Heavenly Father. No matter if you are the greatest sinner, forget it. If you have made up your mind to be good, then you are no longer a sinner....* Start with a clean slate and say: "I have always been good; I was only dreaming that I was bad." It is true: evil is a nightmare and does not belong to the soul.

❖ ❖ ❖

Though your errors be as deep as the ocean, the soul itself cannot be swallowed up by them. Have unflinching determination to move on your path unhampered by limiting thoughts of past errors.

❖ ❖ ❖

* "Even he with the worst of karma who ceaselessly meditates on Me quickly loses the effects of his past bad actions. Becoming a high-souled being, he soon attains perennial peace. Know this for certain: the devotee who puts his trust in Me never perishes!" (Bhagavad Gita IX:30–31).

You are a spark of an Eternal Flame. You can hide the spark, but you can never destroy it.

❖ ❖ ❖

Darkness may reign in a cave for thousands of years, but bring in the light, and the darkness vanishes as though it had never been. Similarly, no matter what your defects, they are yours no longer when you bring in the light of goodness. So great is the light of the soul that incarnations of evil cannot destroy it.

❖ ❖ ❖

No sin is unforgivable, no evil insuperable; for the world of relativity does not contain absolutes.

❖ ❖ ❖

God never forsakes anyone. When, having sinned, you believe your guilt to be measureless, beyond redemption; and when the world declares you of no account and says you will never amount to anything, stop a moment to think of the Divine Mother.* Say to Her, "Divine Mother, I am Your child, Your naughty child. Please forgive me." When you appeal to the mother aspect of God there is no retort — you simply melt the Divine Heart. But God will not support you if you continue to do wrong. You must forsake your evil actions as you pray.

❖ ❖ ❖

Saints are sinners who did not give up. No matter what your difficulties, if you do not give up, you are

* See glossary.

making progress in your struggle against the stream. To struggle is to win the favor of God.

❖ ❖ ❖

Is a diamond less valuable because it is covered with mud? God sees the changeless beauty of our souls. He knows we are not our mistakes.

❖ ❖ ❖

For a few incarnations you have been a human being, but throughout eternity you have been a child of God. Never think of yourself as a sinner, because sin and ignorance are only mortal nightmares. When we will awaken in God, we will find that we — the soul, the pure consciousness — never did anything wrong. Untainted by mortal experiences, we are and ever have been the sons of God.

❖ ❖ ❖

Each of us is a child of God. We are born of His spirit, in all its purity and glory and joy. That heritage is unassailable. To condemn oneself as a sinner, committed to the path of error, is the greatest of all sins. The Bible says: "Know ye not that ye are the temple of God, and that the Spirit of God dwelleth in you?"* Always remember: your Father loves you unconditionally.

* I Corinthians 3:16. Cf. Bhagavad Gita XIII:23, 33: "The Supreme Spirit existing in the body is the detached Beholder, the Consenter, the Sustainer, the Experiencer, the Great Lord, and the Highest Self. …The Self, though seated everywhere in the body, is ever taintless."

Creating Good Habits and Destroying Bad Ones

Turn toward God and you will find yourself shaking off the chains of habits and environment....The Self identified with the ego is bound; the Self identified with the soul is free.

❖ ❖ ❖

The mind may tell you that you cannot free yourself from a particular habit; but habits are nothing but repetitions of your own thoughts, and these you have the capacity to change.

❖ ❖ ❖

Most people who make up their minds to stop smoking or to stop eating so many sweets will continue with those actions in spite of themselves. They do not change because their minds, like blotting paper, have soaked up habits of thought. Habit means that the mind believes it cannot get rid of a particular thought. Habit, indeed, is tenacious. Once you perform an action, it leaves an effect or impression on the consciousness. As a result of this influence, you are likely to repeat that action.

❖ ❖ ❖

Repeated performance of an action creates a mental blueprint. Every action is performed mentally as well as physically, and repetition of a particular action and its accompanying thought-pattern causes the formation of subtle electrical pathways in the physiological brain, somewhat like the grooves in a phonograph record. After a time, whenever you put the needle of attention on those "grooves" of electrical pathways, it plays back the "record" of the original mental blueprint. Each time an action is repeated, these grooves of electrical pathways become deeper, until the slightest attention automatically "plays" those same actions over and over again.

❖ ❖ ❖

These patterns make you behave in a certain way, often against your wish. Your life follows those grooves that you yourself have created in the brain. In that sense you are not a free person; you are more or less a victim of the habits you have formed. Depending on how set those patterns are, to that degree you are a puppet. But you can *neutralize* the dictates of those bad habits. How? By creating brain patterns of opposite good habits. And you can completely *erase* the grooves of bad habits by meditation.

❖ ❖ ❖

You must cure yourself of evil habits by cauterizing them with the opposite good habits. For instance, if you have a bad habit of telling lies and by doing so have lost many friends, start the opposite good habit of telling the truth.

❖ ❖ ❖

Weaken a bad habit by avoiding everything that occasioned it or stimulated it, without concentrating upon it in your zeal to avoid it. Then divert your mind to some good habit and steadily cultivate it until it becomes a dependable part of you.

❖ ❖ ❖

It takes time for even a bad habit to attain supremacy, so why be impatient about the growth of a rival good habit? Do not despair about your undesirable habits; simply stop feeding them and thus making them strong by repetition. The time that elapses in the formation of habits varies with individual nervous systems and brains and is chiefly determined by the quality of attention.

❖ ❖ ❖

Through the power of deep, concentration-trained attention, any habit may be installed—that is, new patterns may be made in the brain—almost instantaneously and at will.

❖ ❖ ❖

When you want to create a good habit or destroy a bad one, concentrate on the brain cells, the storehouse of the mechanisms of habits. To create a good habit, meditate; and then with the concentration fixed at the Christ center, the center of will between the eyebrows, deeply affirm the good habit that you want to install. And when you want to destroy bad habits, concentrate at the Christ center and deeply affirm that all the grooves of bad habits are being erased.

❖ ❖ ❖

By concentration and will power you can erase even deep grooves of long-standing habits. If you are addicted to smoking, for example, say to yourself: "The habit of smoking has long been lodged in my brain. Now I put all my attention and concentration on my brain and I *will* that habit to be dislodged." Command your mind thus, again and again. The best time of the day to do this is in the morning, when the will and attention are fresh. Repeatedly affirm your freedom, using all the strength of your will power. One day you will suddenly feel that you no longer are ensnared by that habit.

❖ ❖ ❖

If you really want to rid yourself of present bad habits...you have no greater recourse than meditation. Every time you meditate deeply on God, beneficial changes take place in the patterns of your brain.

❖ ❖ ❖

Meditate upon the thought, "I and my Father are one," trying to feel a great peace, and then a great joy in your heart. When that joy comes, say, "Father, Thou art with me. I command Thy power within me to cauterize my brain cells of wrong habits and past seed tendencies." The power of God in meditation will do it. Rid yourself of the limiting consciousness that you are a man or a woman; *know* that you are the child of God. Then mentally affirm and pray to God: "I command my brain cells to change, to destroy the grooves of bad habits that have made a puppet out of me. Lord, burn them up in Thy divine light."

❖ ❖ ❖

Suppose your problem is that you frequently get angry, and afterwards feel very sorry for having lost your temper. Every night and morning make up your mind to avoid anger, and then watch yourself carefully. The first day may be difficult, but the second may be a little easier. The third will be easier still. After a few days you will see that victory is possible. In a year, if you keep up your effort, you will be another person.

Prayer for Discriminative Wisdom

Give me the wisdom to follow happily the ways of righteousness. May I develop the soul faculty of discrimination that detects evil, in even its subtlest forms; and that guides me to the humble paths of goodness.

Affirmation for Removing Bad Habits

[Paramahansa Yogananda concluded one of his public talks on overcoming habits by addressing his listeners as follows:]

Close your eyes and think of one bad habit you want to get rid of.... Affirm with me: "I am free of that habit now! I am free!" Hold on to that thought of freedom; forget the bad habit.

Repeat after me, "I shall remold my consciousness. In this new year I am a new person. And I shall change my consciousness again and again until I have driven away all the darkness of ignorance and manifested the shining light of Spirit in whose image I am made."

Prayer

O Divine Teacher, let me realize that though the gloom of my ignorance be age-old, with the dawn of Thy light the darkness will vanish as though it had never been.

CHAPTER 9

Happiness

If you have given up hope of ever being happy, cheer up. Never lose hope. Your soul, being a reflection of the ever joyous Spirit, is, in essence, happiness itself.

❖ ❖ ❖

If it is happiness you want, have it! There is nothing that can stop you.

Positive Mental Attitudes

Happiness depends to some extent upon external conditions, but chiefly upon mental attitudes.

❖ ❖ ❖

Essentially, conditions are neither good nor bad; they are always neutral, seeming to be either depressing or encouraging because of the sad or bright attitude of the mind of the individual concerned with them.

❖ ❖ ❖

Change your thoughts if you wish to change your circumstances. Since you alone are responsible for your thoughts, only you can change them. You will want to change them when you realize that each thought creates according to its own nature. Remember that the law works at all times and that you are always demonstrating according to the kind of thoughts you habitually entertain. Therefore, start now to think only those thoughts that will bring you health and happiness.

❖ ❖ ❖

Man needs to understand that his own intelligence controls the atoms of his body. He should not live in a closed chamber of mental narrowness. Breathe in the fresh air of vital thoughts and views of other people. Expel poisonous thoughts of discouragement, discontentment, hopelessness. Drink vitality and receive mental nourishment from materially and spiritually progressive minds. Feast unstintingly on the creative thinking within yourself and others. Take long mental walks on the path of self-confidence. Exercise with the instruments of judgment, introspection, and initiative.

❖ ❖ ❖

The mind, being the brain, feeling, and perception of all living cells, can keep the human body alert or depressed. The mind is the king, and all its cellular subjects behave exactly according to the mood of their royal master. Just as we concern ourselves with the nutritive value of our daily food menus, so should we consider the nutritive potency of the psychological menus that we daily serve the mind.

❖ ❖ ❖

Constantly you affirm sorrow, therefore it exists. Deny it in your mind and it will exist no longer. This assertion of the Self is what I call the hero in man. It is his divine or essential nature. In order to acquire freedom from sorrow, man must assert his heroic self in all his daily activities.

❖ ❖ ❖

If you do not choose to be happy no one can make you happy. Do not blame God for that! And if you choose to be happy, no one can make you unhappy. If He had not given us freedom to use our own will, we could blame Him when we are unhappy, but He did give us that freedom. It is we who make of life what it is.

❖ ❖ ❖

Often we continue to suffer without making an effort to change; that is why we don't find lasting peace and contentment. If we would persevere we would certainly be able to conquer all difficulties. We must make the effort, that we may go from misery to happiness, from despondency to courage.

❖ ❖ ❖

The root of sorrow lies in the dearth of heroism and courage in the character of the average man. When the heroic element is lacking in the mental makeup of a person, his mind becomes susceptible to the threat of all passing sorrows.

❖ ❖ ❖

Persons of strong character are usually the happiest. They do not blame others for troubles that can usually be traced to their own actions and lack of understanding. They know that no one has any power to add to their happiness or detract from it unless they themselves are so weak that they allow the adverse thoughts and wicked actions of others to affect them.

❖ ❖ ❖

As long as the conqueror in man is awake, no sorrow can cast its shadow over the threshold of his heart.... Awaken the victor in yourself, arouse the sleeping hero in yourself, and lo! no sorrow will ever again overwhelm you.

❖ ❖ ❖

Your highest happiness lies in your being ever ready in desiring to learn, and to behave properly. The more you improve yourself, the more you will elevate others around you. The self-improving man is the increasingly happy man. The happier you become, the happier will be the people around you.

❖ ❖ ❖

Avoid a negative approach to life. Why gaze down the sewers when there is loveliness all around us? One may find some fault in even the greatest masterpieces of art, music, and literature. But isn't it better to enjoy their charm and glory?

❖ ❖ ❖

Nearly everyone is familiar with those three little monkey-figures that depict the maxim, "See no evil, hear no evil, speak no evil." I emphasize the positive approach: "See that which is good, hear that which is good, speak that which is good."

❖ ❖ ❖

Good and evil, the positive and the negative, both exist in this world. While trying to keep the consciousness positive, many people become unreasonably afraid of negative thoughts. It is useless to deny that negative thoughts exist, but neither should you fear them. Use your discrimination to analyze wrong thoughts; and then dump them.

❖ ❖ ❖

Life has a bright side and a dark side, for the world of relativity is composed of light and shadows. If you permit your thoughts to dwell on evil, you yourself will become ugly. Look only for the good in everything, that you absorb the quality of beauty.

❖ ❖ ❖

Thinking, reading, and repeating statements of truth with deep attention will help to clear away negation and to establish a positive attitude in your mind. Repeat your prayers and affirmations with deep concentration until you establish a habit of thought, until it becomes as natural for you to think in the right way as it previously was for you to think negatively.

Freedom From Negative Moods

The ever new joy of God inherent in the soul is indestructible. So also, its expression in the mind can never be destroyed if one knows how to hold on to it, and if he does not deliberately change his mind and become sorrowful by nurturing moods.

❖ ❖ ❖

You are an image of God; you should behave like a god. But what happens? First thing in the morning you lose your temper and complain, "My coffee is cold!" What does it matter? Why be disturbed by such things? Have that evenness of mind wherein you are absolutely calm, free from all anger. That is what you want. Don't let anyone or anything "get your goat." Your "goat" is your peace. Let nothing take it away from you.

❖ ❖ ❖

Resurrect yourself from the littleness of life, the little things that disturb you.

❖ ❖ ❖

Nobody *likes* misery. Why not analyze yourself next time you are in a mood? You will see how you are willingly, willfully making yourself miserable. And while you are doing so, others around you feel the unpleasantness of your state of mind....You must remove moods from your mental mirror.

❖ ❖ ❖

Always think of your mind as a garden, and keep it beautiful and fragrant with divine thoughts; let it not become a mud pond, rank with malodorous hateful moods. If you cultivate the heavenly scented blooms of peace and love, the bee of Christ Consciousness* will steal into your garden. As the bee seeks out only those flowers that are sweet with honey, so God

---

* God's consciousness, omnipresent in creation. See glossary.

comes only when your life is sweet with honeyed thoughts.

❖ ❖ ❖

Each type of mood has a specific cause, and it lies within your own mind.

❖ ❖ ❖

One should introspect each day in order to understand the nature of his mood, and how to correct it, if it is a harmful one. Perhaps you find yourself in an indifferent state of mind. No matter what is suggested, you are not interested. It is necessary then to make a conscious effort to create some positive interest. Beware of indifference, which ossifies your progress in life by paralyzing your will power.

Perhaps your mood is discouragement over sickness; a feeling that you will never regain health. You must try to apply the laws of right living that lead to a healthy, active, and moral life, and pray for greater faith in the healing power of God.

Or suppose your mood is a conviction that you are a failure, and can never succeed at anything. Analyze the problem and see if you have really made all the effort you could have.

❖ ❖ ❖

You can conquer your moods, no matter how terrible they seem. Make up your mind that you are not going to be moody anymore; and if a mood comes in spite of your resolve, analyze the cause that brought it on, and do something constructive about it.

❖ ❖ ❖

Creative thinking* is the best antidote for moods. Moods get their grip on your consciousness when you are in a negative or passive state of mind. The time when your mind is vacant is just the time it can become moody; and when you are moody, the devil comes and wields his influence on you. Therefore, develop creative thinking. Whenever you are not active physically, do something creative in your mind. Keep it so busy that you have no time to indulge in moodiness.

❖ ❖ ❖

When you are thinking creatively, you don't feel the body or moods; you become attuned with Spirit. Our human intelligence is made in the image of His creative intelligence, through which all things are possible; and if we don't live in that consciousness, we become a bundle of moods. By thinking creatively we destroy those moods.

❖ ❖ ❖

Remember that when you are unhappy it is generally because you do not visualize strongly enough the great things that you definitely want to accomplish in life, nor do you employ steadfastly enough your will power, your creative ability, and your patience until your dreams are materialized.

❖ ❖ ❖

* See also pages 62–66.

Keep busy doing constructive things for your own self-improvement and for the benefit of others, for whoever would enter God's kingdom must try also to do good for others every day. If you follow this pattern, you will feel the mood-dispelling joy of knowing you are advancing, mentally, physically, and spiritually.

Service to Others

Happiness lies in making others happy, in forsaking self-interest to bring joy to others.

❖ ❖ ❖

Giving happiness to others is tremendously important to our own happiness, and a most satisfying experience. Some people think only of their own family: "Us four and no more." Others think only of self: "How am *I* going to be happy?" But these are the very persons who do not become happy!

❖ ❖ ❖

To live for self is the source of all misery.

❖ ❖ ❖

In being of spiritual, mental, and material service to others, you will find your own needs fulfilled. As you forget *self* in service to others, you will find that, without seeking it, your own cup of happiness will be full.

❖ ❖ ❖

When you came into this world, you cried and everyone else smiled. You should so live your life that when you leave, everyone else will cry, but you will be smiling.

❖ ❖ ❖

The deeper you meditate and the more willingly you serve, the happier you will be.

The Inner Conditions of Happiness

Learn to carry all the conditions of happiness within yourself by meditating and attuning your consciousness to the ever-existing, ever-conscious, ever-new Joy, which is God. Your happiness should never be subject to any outside influence. Whatever your environment is, don't allow your inner peace to be touched by it.

❖ ❖ ❖

When you have mastery of your feelings you abide in your true state. The true state of the Self, the soul, is bliss, wisdom, love, peace. It is to be so happy that no matter what you are doing you enjoy it. Isn't that much better than to blunder through the world like a restless demon, unable to find satisfaction in anything? When centered in your true self, you do every task and enjoy all good things with the joy of God. Filled with His intoxicating bliss, you joyfully perform all actions.

❖ ❖ ❖

In the spiritual life one becomes just like a little child — without resentment, without attachment, full of life and joy.

❖ ❖ ❖

Real happiness can stand the challenge of all outer experiences. When you can bear the crucifixions of others' wrongs against you and still return love and forgiveness; and when you can keep that divine inner peace intact despite all painful thrusts of outer circumstance, then you shall know this happiness.

❖ ❖ ❖

Be silent and calm [in meditation] every night for at least half an hour, preferably much longer, before you retire, and again in the morning before starting the day's activity. This will produce an undaunted, unbreakable inner habit of happiness that will make you able to meet all the trying situations of the everyday battle of life. With that unchangeable happiness within, go about seeking to fulfill the demands of your daily needs.

❖ ❖ ❖

If you keep the eyes of your concentration closed, you cannot see the sun of happiness burning within your bosom; but no matter how tightly you close the eyes of your attention, the fact nevertheless remains that the happiness rays are ever trying to pierce the closed doors of your mind. Open the windows of calmness and you will find a sudden burst of the bright sun of joy within your very Self.

❖ ❖ ❖

The joyous rays of the soul may be perceived if you interiorize your attention. These perceptions may be had by training your mind to enjoy the beautiful scenery of thoughts in the invisible, intangible kingdom within you. Do not search for happiness only in beautiful clothes, clean houses, delicious dinners, soft cushions, and luxuries. These will imprison your happiness behind the bars of externality, of outwardness.

❖ ❖ ❖

I appreciate whatever God gives me, but I don't miss it when it is gone. Someone once gave me a beautiful coat and hat, an expensive outfit. Then began my worry. I had to be concerned about not tearing or soiling it. It made me uncomfortable. I said, "Lord, why did You give me this bother?" One day I was to lecture in Trinity Hall here in Los Angeles. When I arrived at the hall and started to remove my coat, the Lord told me, "Take away your belongings from the pockets." I did so. When I returned to the cloakroom after my lecture, the coat was gone. I was angry, and someone said, "Never mind, we will get you another coat." I replied, "I am not angry because I lost the coat, but because whoever took it didn't take the hat that matches it, too!"

Don't let your feelings rule you. How can you be happy if you are all the time fussing about your clothes or other possessions? Dress neatly in clean clothes and then forget about them; clean your house and forget it.

❖ ❖ ❖

The more you depend upon conditions outside yourself for happiness, the less happiness you will experience.

❖ ❖ ❖

If you think that you can live happily in forgetfulness of God, you are mistaken, because you will

cry out in loneliness again and again until you realize
that God is all in all—the only reality in the universe.
You are made in His image. You can never find lasting
happiness in any *thing* because nothing is complete
except God.

❖ ❖ ❖

The unalloyed happiness I find in communion
with the Lord no words can describe. Night and day
I am in a state of joy. That joy is God. To know Him
is to perform the funeral rites for all your sorrows. He
does not require you to be stoic and morose. This is
not the right concept of God, nor the way to please
Him. Without being happy you will not even be able
to find Him....The happier you are, the greater will
be your attunement with Him. Those who know Him
are always happy, because God is joy itself.

Affirmations

*Beginning with the early dawn, I will radiate
my cheer to everyone I meet today. I will be
the mental sunshine for all who cross my path
this day.*

❖ ❖ ❖

*I form new habits of thinking by seeing the
good everywhere, and by beholding all things
as the perfect idea of God made manifest.*

❖ ❖ ❖

*I will make up my mind to be happy within
myself right now, where I am today.*

CHAPTER 10

Getting Along With Others

The greatest of all happiness, next to divine happiness, is to be at peace with one's immediate relations, those with whom one must live every day in the year. When people try to handle the extremely complicated machinery of human feelings without any training whatsoever, the consequent results are often disastrous. Very few persons realize that most of our happiness lies in the art of understanding the law of human behavior. That is why so many people are often "in hot water" with their friends, and, worse yet, at constant war with their own best beloved ones at home.

Dealing With Inharmonious Relationships

The basic law of right human behavior is self-reform . . . . Whenever any trouble occurs with our friends or dear ones, we should inwardly lay the blame on ourselves for getting into an unpleasant situation and then try to get out of it as fast and as graciously as we can. It is fruitless to increase the trouble by loudly, unkindly, discourteously blaming others, even though we find that they are to blame. We can teach quick-tempered dear ones to mend their faults a hundred times better by setting a good example than we can by harsh or self-righteous words.

❖ ❖ ❖

When there is a fight, at least two parties are involved. So there can be no fight with you if you refuse to participate.

❖ ❖ ❖

If someone speaks to you in hurtful language, remain quiet; or say, "I am sorry if I have done something to offend you," and then remain silent.

❖ ❖ ❖

The spiritual man conquers wrath by calmness, stops quarrels by keeping silence, dispels inharmony by being sweet of speech, and shames discourtesy by being thoughtful of others.

❖ ❖ ❖

There is no more liberating action than sincerely to give people kindness in return for unkindness.

❖ ❖ ❖

Never be mean. Have resentment toward none. I prefer some sinners with good hearts to some socalled good people who are bigoted and uncompassionate. To be spiritual is to be broad, to understand and forgive, and to be a friend to all.

❖ ❖ ❖

The entire Roman government could not have roused unkindness in Christ. Even for those who crucified him, he prayed: "Father, forgive them; for they know not what they do."*

❖ ❖ ❖

* Luke 23:34.

Inward civility, inner heartfelt courtesy, and continuous goodwill are the proper panaceas for all bad behavior.

❖ ❖ ❖

Most of the time, people talk and act from their own viewpoint. They seldom see, or even try to see, the other person's side. If, lacking understanding, you enter into a fight with someone, remember that each of you is as much to blame as the other, regardless of which one started the argument. "Fools argue; wise men discuss."

❖ ❖ ❖

To have calm feeling doesn't mean that you always smile and agree with everyone no matter what they say — that you regard truth but don't want to annoy anybody with it. This is going to the extreme. Those who try in this way to please everyone, with the desire of getting praise for their good nature, do not necessarily have control of feeling....Whoever has control of feeling follows truth, shares that truth wherever he can, and avoids annoying unnecessarily anyone who would not be receptive anyway. He knows when to speak and when to be silent, but he never compromises his own ideals and inner peace. Such a man is a force for great good in this world.

❖ ❖ ❖

We should make ourselves attractive by wearing the fine garment of genuinely courteous language. We should first of all be courteous to our immediate relatives. When one can do that, he will be habitually kind to all people. Real family happiness has its foundation on the altar of understanding and kind words. It is not necessary to agree on everything in order to show kindness. Calm silence, sincerity, and courteous words, whether one is agreeing or disagreeing with others, mark the person who knows how to behave.

❖ ❖ ❖

If you want to be loved, start loving others who need your love....If you want others to sympathize with you, start showing sympathy to those around you. If you want to be respected, you must learn to be respectful to everyone, both young and old....Whatever you want others to be, first be that yourself; then you will find others responding in like manner to you.

Developing a Harmonious Personality

Be genuinely amiable when you are with others. Never be a "sourpuss." You don't have to laugh boisterously, like a hyena, but don't wear a long face either. Just be smiling, congenial, and kind. Smiling on the outside when you are angry or resentful inside, however, is hypocrisy. If you want to be likable, be sincere. Sincerity is a soul quality that God has given to every human being, but not all express it. Above all, be humble. Though you may have admirable inner strength, don't overwhelm others with your strong nature. Be calm and considerate of them. This is the way to develop likable magnetism.

❖ ❖ ❖

Don't try to get along with others by adopting artificial mannerisms. Just be loving and ever ready to be helpful and saturate yourself with divine communion—then you will find yourself getting along with everyone in your environment.

❖ ❖ ❖

In your relationships with others, it is extremely necessary to recognize and appreciate the characteristics that they have chiseled out in themselves. If you study people with an open mind, you will better understand them and be able to get along with them. You will instantly be able to tell what kind of person you are dealing with and know how to deal with him. Don't talk to a philosopher about horse racing, or to a scientist about housekeeping. Find out what interests an individual, and then talk with him about that subject, not necessarily what interests you.

❖ ❖ ❖

When you talk, don't talk too much about yourself. Try to speak on a subject that interests the other person. And listen. That is the way to be attractive. You will see how your presence is in demand.

❖ ❖ ❖

An inferiority complex is born of a secret awareness of real or imagined weaknesses. In trying to compensate for such weaknesses, a person may build an armor of false pride, and exhibit an inflated ego. Then those who do not understand the real cause of such an attitude may say the person has a superiority complex. Both manifestations of his inner inharmony are destructive to Self-development. Both are fostered by imagination and by ignoring facts, while neither belongs to the true, all-powerful nature of the soul. Found your self-confidence upon actual achievements plus the knowledge that your real Self (the soul) can never be "inferior" in any way; then you will be free from all complexes.

❖ ❖ ❖

If the majority find you an unattractive personality, analyze yourself. There may be some traits in your make-up that are repugnant to others. Perhaps you talk too much, or you make it a practice to put your finger into everyone else's pie, or you have the habit of telling others what is wrong with them and how they should lead their lives, and you won't accept any suggestions for improving yourself. These are examples of psychological characteristics that make us unattractive to others.

❖ ❖ ❖

Consideration for others is a most wonderful quality. It is the greatest attractiveness you can have. Practice it! If someone is thirsty, a thoughtful person anticipates his need and offers him a drink. Consideration means awareness of and attentiveness to others. A considerate person, when in the company of others, will have an intuitive awareness of their needs.

❖ ❖ ❖

Practice consideration and goodness until you are like a beautiful flower that everyone loves to see. Be the beauty that is in a flower, and the attractiveness that is in a pure mind. When you are attractive in that way, you will always have true friends. You will be loved by both man and God.

Overcoming Negative Emotions

Whatever you give out will come back to you. Hate, and you will receive hate in return. When you fill yourself with inharmonious thoughts and emotions, you are destroying yourself. Why hate or be angry with anyone? Love your enemies. Why stew in the heat of anger? If you become riled, get over it at once. Take a walk, count to ten or fifteen, or divert your mind to something pleasant. Let go of the desire to retaliate. When you are angry your brain is overheating, your heart is having valve trouble, your whole body is being devitalized. Exude peace and goodness; because that is the nature of the image of God within you—your true nature. Then no one can disturb you.

❖ ❖ ❖

Whenever you are jealous, you are in collusion with the cosmic delusion of Satan.* Whenever you are angry, Satan is guiding you....Any time the voice of jealousy, fear, or anger speaks, remember that it is not your voice, and command that it be gone. But you will not be able to expel that evil, no matter how you

* See *maya* in glossary.

try, so long as you give that negative feeling a safe harbor in your mind. Eradicate jealousy, fear, and anger from within, so that every time an evil impulse tells you to hate and to hurt, another stronger voice within tells you to love and to forgive. Listen to *that* voice.

❖ ❖ ❖

Jealousy comes from an inferiority complex, and expresses itself through suspicion and fear. It signifies that a person is afraid he cannot hold his own in his relationships with others, be they conjugal, filial, social. If you feel you have cause to be jealous of someone—for example, if you are afraid that the one you love is transferring his or her attention to another—first strive to understand if there is something lacking within yourself. Improve yourself; develop yourself. The only way to hold on to the affection or respect of another is to apply the law of love and to merit that recognition by self-improvement.... Fulfillment lies in constantly improving yourself so that instead of your seeking others, others will seek you.

❖ ❖ ❖

Even while striving to improve yourself, learn to stand alone, secure in your own virtues and self-worth. If you want others to believe in you, remember, it isn't only your words that have an effect, but what you are and what you feel within—what is in your soul. Always strive to be an angel within, no matter how others behave. Be sincere, kind, loving, and understanding.

❖ ❖ ❖

When someone comes to you in anger, remain in charge of yourself. "I will not lose my temper. I will keep on expressing calmness until his feeling changes."

❖ ❖ ❖

When a loved one ... tries our patience beyond endurance, we should retire to a quiet place, lock the door, practice some physical exercise, and then quiet ourselves in the following way:

Sit in a straight chair, with spine erect; slowly inhale and exhale, twelve times. Then deeply affirm mentally, ten times or more: "Father, Thou art harmony. Let me reflect Thy harmony. Harmonize my error-stricken dear one."

One should affirm this until he feels, through the deep sense of peace and calm assurance falling upon him, that God has heard him and has answered.

❖ ❖ ❖

"Aren't your teachings about controlling the emotions dangerous?" a student asked. "Many psychologists claim that suppression leads to mental maladjustments and even to physical illness."

Paramahansa Yogananda replied: "Suppression is harmful—holding the thought that you want something but doing nothing constructive to get it. Self-control is beneficial — patiently replacing wrong thoughts by right ones, changing reprehensible actions to helpful ones.

"Those who dwell on evil hurt themselves. Men who fill their minds with wisdom and their lives with constructive activities spare themselves ignoble suffering."

❖ ❖ ❖

"Wrath springs only from thwarted desires," [Sri Yukteswar said]. "I do not expect anything from others, so their actions cannot be in opposition to wishes of mine."

❖ ❖ ❖

If someone hurts you deeply, you remember it. But instead of concentrating on that, you should think of all the good things about the person who has hurt you, and of all the goodness that you have in your life. Don't take notice of the insults people give you.

❖ ❖ ❖

Concentrate on trying to behold God in your enemy; for by doing so you release yourself from evil vengeful desires that destroy your peace of mind. By heaping hatred upon hatred, or giving hate in return for hate, you not only increase your enemy's hostility toward you; you poison your system, physically as well as emotionally, with your own venom.

❖ ❖ ❖

Have only love in your heart for others. The more you see the good in them, the more you will establish good in yourself. Hold the consciousness of good. The way to make people good is to see the good in them. Do not nag them. Remain calm, serene, always in command of yourself. You will then find out how easy it is to get along.

❖ ❖ ❖

Cleanse your mind of all adverse criticism of others. Use a look or a hint to correct lovingly a receptive person, but do not force correction, and do not continue to hold critical thoughts, even though you remain silent.

❖ ❖ ❖

Thoughts can sometimes be more effective than words. The human mind is the most powerful broadcasting machine there is. If you constantly broadcast positive thoughts with love, those thoughts will have an effect on others. (Similarly, if you broadcast jealousy or hatred, others receive those thoughts and respond accordingly.) Ask God to put His power behind your efforts. If, for instance, it is the husband that is going astray, the wife should pray to God: "Lord, help me to help my husband. Keep all taint of jealousy and resentment out of my heart. I only pray that he realize his error and change. Lord, be with him; and bless me that I do my part." If your communion with God is deep, you will see that person change.

❖ ❖ ❖

It is easy to strike back, but to give love is the highest way to try to disarm your persecutor. Even if it doesn't work at the time, he will never be able to forget that when he gave you a slap, you gave love in return. That love must be sincere; when it comes from the heart, love is magical. You should not look for the effects; even if your love is spurned, pay no attention. Give love and forget. Don't expect anything; then you will see the magical result.

Forgiveness

The God of some scriptures is a revengeful deity, always ready to punish us. But Jesus showed us the real nature of God . . . . He did not destroy his enemies with "twelve legions of angels,"* but rather overcame evil with the power of divine love. His actions demonstrated the supreme love of God, and the behavior of those who are one with Him.

❖ ❖ ❖

"One should forgive, under any injury," says the *Mahabharata.*† "It hath been said that the continuation of the species is due to man's being forgiving. Forgiveness is holiness; by forgiveness the universe is held together. Forgiveness is the might of the mighty; forgiveness is sacrifice; forgiveness is quiet of mind. Forgiveness and gentleness are the qualities of the Self-possessed. They represent eternal virtue."

❖ ❖ ❖

"Then came Peter to him and said, Lord, how oft shall my brother sin against me, and I forgive him? till seven times? Jesus saith unto him, I say not unto thee, Until seven times: but, Until seventy times seven."‡ I prayed deeply to understand this uncompromising counsel. "Lord," I protested, "is it possible?"

---

* "Thinkest thou that I cannot now pray to my Father, and he shall presently give me more than twelve legions of angels?" (Matthew 26:53).

† A great epic scripture of India, of which the Bhagavad Gita is a part.

‡ Matthew 18:21–22.

When the Divine Voice finally responded, It brought
a humbling flood of light: "How many times, O Man,
do I forgive each of you daily?"

❖ ❖ ❖

As God is constantly forgiving us, even knowing
all our [wrong] thoughts, so those who are fully in
tune with Him naturally have that same love.

❖ ❖ ❖

In your heart must well that sympathy which
soothes away all pains from the hearts of others, that
sympathy which enabled Jesus to say: "Father, forgive
them; for they know not what they do."* His great
love encompassed all. He could have destroyed his
enemies with a look, yet just as God is constantly forgiving us even though He knows all our wicked
thoughts, so those great souls who are in tune with
Him give us that same love.

❖ ❖ ❖

If you would develop Christ-consciousness,†
learn to be sympathetic. When genuine feeling for
others comes into your heart, you are beginning to
manifest that great consciousness....Lord Krishna
said: "He is a supreme yogi who regards with equal-
mindedness all men...."‡

❖ ❖ ❖

* Luke 23:34.
† Universal consciousness; oneness with the omnipresence of God.
See glossary.
‡ Bhagavad Gita VI:9.

Wrath and hatred accomplish nothing. Love rewards. You may cow down someone, but once that person has risen again, he will try to destroy you. Then how have you conquered him? You have not. The only way to conquer is by love. And where you cannot conquer, just be silent or get away, and pray for him. That is the way you must love. If you practice this in your life, you will have peace beyond understanding.

Affirmation

I will try to please everyone by kind, considerate actions, ever striving to remove any misunderstanding knowingly or unknowingly caused by me.

❖ ❖ ❖

Today I forgive all those who have ever offended me. I give my love to all thirsty hearts, both to those who love me and those who do not love me.

CHAPTER 11

Unconditional Love: Perfecting Human Relationships

The world as a whole has forgotten the real meaning of the word *love*. Love has been so abused and crucified by man that very few people know what true love is. Just as oil is present in every part of the olive, so love permeates every part of creation. But to define love is very difficult, for the same reason that words cannot fully describe the flavor of an orange. You have to taste the fruit to know its flavor. So with love.

❖ ❖ ❖

In the universal sense, love is the divine power of attraction in creation that harmonizes, unites, binds together....Those who live in tune with the attractive force of love achieve harmony with nature and their fellow beings, and are attracted to blissful reunion with God.

❖ ❖ ❖

"Ordinary love is selfish, darkly rooted in desires and satisfactions," [Sri Yukteswar said]. "Divine love is without condition, without boundary, without change. The flux of the human heart is gone forever at the transfixing touch of pure love."

❖ ❖ ❖

Many human beings say "I love you" one day and reject you the next. That is not love. One whose heart is filled with the love of God cannot willfully hurt anyone. When you love God without reservation, He fills your heart with His unconditional love for all. That love no human tongue can describe....The ordinary man is incapable of loving others in this way. Self-centered in the consciousness of "I, me, and mine," he has not yet discovered the omnipresent God who resides in him and in all other beings. To me there is no difference between one person and another; I behold all as soul-reflections of the one God. I can't think of anyone as a stranger, for I know that we are all part of the One Spirit. When you experience the true meaning of religion, which is to know God, you will realize that He is your Self, and that He exists equally and impartially in all beings. Then you will be able to love others as your own Self.*

❖ ❖ ❖

In the consciousness of one who is immersed in the divine love of God, there is no deception, no narrowness of caste or creed, no boundaries of any kind. When you experience that divine love, you will see no difference between flower and beast, between one human being and another. You will commune with all nature, and you will love equally all mankind.

❖ ❖ ❖

* "Thou shalt love the Lord thy God with all thy heart, and with all thy soul, and with all thy strength, and with all thy mind; and thy neighbor as thyself" (Luke 10:27).

Compassion toward all beings is necessary for divine realization, for God Himself is overflowing with this quality. Those with a tender heart can put themselves in the place of others, feel their suffering, and try to alleviate it.*

Balancing Feminine and Masculine Qualities

It seems there has always been a rivalry between man and woman. But they are equals; neither one is superior. Be proud of what you are in this life.

❖ ❖ ❖

"In sleep, you do not know whether you are a man or a woman," [Sri Yukteswar said]. "Just as a man, impersonating a woman, does not become one, so the soul, impersonating both man and woman, remains changeless. The soul is the immutable, unqualified image of God."

❖ ❖ ❖

Do not even allow yourself to be limited to the consciousness that you are a man or a woman: You are a soul made in God's image....The wisest course is to remember always, "I am neither man nor woman; I am Spirit." Then you will rid yourself of the limiting consciousness of both tendencies; you will realize your highest divine potential, whether you are incarnate as a man or a woman.

---

* Lord Krishna taught: "The best type of yogi is he who feels for others, whether in grief or pleasure, even as he feels for himself" (Bhagavad Gita VI:32).

❖ ❖ ❖

God is both infinite wisdom and infinite feeling. When He manifested Himself in creation, God gave His wisdom a form in the father; and He gave His feeling a form in the mother.... Every father and every mother is potentially endowed with both the fatherly wisdom and the motherly tenderness of God. They have to perfect these endowments....The divine man develops both the fatherly and motherly qualities in himself.

❖ ❖ ❖

Man argues that woman is emotional and cannot reason; and woman complains that man cannot feel. Both are incorrect. Woman can reason, but feeling is uppermost in her nature; and man can feel, but in him reason is predominant.

❖ ❖ ❖

God created these physiological and mental differences in order to make some distinction between man and woman. The ideal spiritual union between them was meant to bring out the hidden feeling in man and to develop the hidden reason in woman. They were meant to aid each other in developing the pure divine qualities of perfect reason and feeling.

❖ ❖ ❖

Each sex should strive toward a balance by learning from one another through friendship and understanding.

❖ ❖ ❖

Unless man and woman understand each other's nature, they ignorantly torture one another....Each should strive for an inner balance of both reason and feeling, and so become a "whole" personality, a perfected human being.

❖ ❖ ❖

By God-communion you bring about the harmony or balance of these two qualities within yourself.

❖ ❖ ❖

In the great saints we see combined the ideal masculine and feminine qualities. Jesus was like that; so were all the masters. When you have attained that perfect reason-feeling equilibrium, you will have learned one of the major lessons for which you were sent here.

❖ ❖ ❖

Mankind must realize that the basic nature of the soul is spiritual. For man and woman to look upon each other only as a means to satisfy lust is to court the destruction of happiness. Slowly, bit by bit, peace of mind will go.

❖ ❖ ❖

Man should strive to see the God in woman, and to help her realize her spiritual nature. He should make her feel that she is with him not merely to satisfy his sensual appetite, but as a companion whom he respects and regards as an expression of the Divine. And woman should look upon man in the same way.

❖ ❖ ❖

When man and woman genuinely and purely love one another, there is complete harmony between them in body, mind, and soul. When their love is expressed in its highest form, it results in a perfect unity.

Marriage

Two persons who unite their lives to help each other toward divine realization are founding their marriage on the right basis: unconditional friendship.

❖ ❖ ❖

To develop pure and unconditional love between husband and wife, parent and child, friend and friend, self and all, is the lesson we have come on earth to learn.

❖ ❖ ❖

True marriage is a laboratory in which poisons of selfishness, bad temper, and bad behavior may be poured into the test tube of patience and neutralized and changed by the catalytic power of love and constant effort to behave nobly.

❖ ❖ ❖

If there is a habit or quality in your mate that rouses unlovely traits in your disposition, you should realize the purpose of this circumstance: to bring to the surface those poisons hidden within you so that you may eliminate them and thus purify your nature.

❖ ❖ ❖

The greatest thing a husband or wife can wish for the spouse is spirituality; for soul unfoldment brings out the divine qualities of understanding, patience, thoughtfulness, love. But each should remember that the desire for spiritual growth cannot be forced on the other. Live love yourself, and your goodness will inspire all your loved ones.

❖ ❖ ❖

Unless married couples keep in mind the true high purpose of marriage, they may never enjoy a really happy life together. Oversexuality, too much familiarity, lack of courtesy, suspiciousness, insulting speech or acts, arguing before children or guests, crankiness, and unloading of troubles or anger on one's mate should be disallowed if marriage is to be ideal.

❖ ❖ ❖

The *first* and most essential requirement for a happy marriage is soul unity—similarity of spiritual ideals and goals, implemented by a practical willingness to attain those goals by study, effort, and self-discipline. Couples who possess soul unity will be able to make a success of marriage even if no other desirable basis is present.

The *second* requirement for a happy marriage is similarity of interest — intellectual, social, environmental, and so on.

The *third*, and last in importance (though usually given first place by unenlightened people), is physical attraction. That bond soon loses its attractive power if the first requirement, or the first and second requirements, are not also present.

❖ ❖ ❖

People who want to marry should first have to learn to control their emotions.* Two people placed together in the arena of marriage without this training battle worse than opponents in a World War! Wars, at least, come to an end after a time; but some marital partners engage in combat throughout life. You would think that in a civilized society people should know how to get along, but few have learned this art. A marriage should be nurtured on high ideals and the wine of God's inspiration; then it will be a happy and mutually beneficial union.

❖ ❖ ❖

If husbands and wives who are accustomed to using each other for target practice, using bullets of wrathful language and discourtesies, would try instead to entertain each other with the soul-solacing charm of kind words, they would then create a new happiness in family life.

❖ ❖ ❖

Sex has its place in the marital relationship between man and woman. But if it becomes the supreme factor in that relationship, love flies out the door and disappears completely; in its place come possessiveness, over-familiarity, and the abuse and loss of friendship and understanding. Though sexual attraction is one of the conditions under which love is born, sex in itself is not love. Sex and love are as

* See also pages 124 ff.

far apart as the moon and the sun. It is only when the transmuting quality of true love is uppermost in the relationship that sex becomes a means of expressing love. Those who live too much on the sex plane lose their way and fail to find a satisfying marital relationship. It is by self-control, in which sex is not the ruling emotion, but only incidental to love, that husband and wife can know what real love is. In this modern world, unfortunately, love is too often destroyed by overemphasis on sex experience.

❖ ❖ ❖

Those who practice a natural—not forced—moderation in their sex life develop other enduring qualities in the husband-wife relationship: friendship, companionship, understanding, mutual love. For example, Madame Amelita Galli-Curci* and her husband, Homer Samuels, are the greatest lovers I have met in the West. Their love is beautiful because they practice these ideals of which I speak. When parted even for a short time, they eagerly look forward to seeing each other again, to being in each other's company, to sharing their thoughts and love.

❖ ❖ ❖

Every individual needs a period of aloneness or solitude in order to cope with the increasing pres-

* World-renowned opera singer (1889–1963) who met Paramahansa Yogananda during his early years in the United States. She and her husband became devoted members of Self-Realization Fellowship. Madame Galli-Curci wrote the foreword to Paramahansa Yogananda's book *Whispers from Eternity*.

sures of life....Do not encroach upon one another's independence.

❖ ❖ ❖

When the husband serves the wife, and she serves him, each with the desire to see the other happy, Christ Consciousness — God's loving Cosmic Intelligence that permeates every atom of creation — has begun to express itself through their consciousness.

❖ ❖ ❖

When two people feel an unconditional attraction for each other, and are ready to sacrifice for one another, they are truly in love.

❖ ❖ ❖

To wish for perfection for the loved one, and to feel pure joy in thinking of that soul, is divine love; and that is the love of true friendship.

❖ ❖ ❖

Meditate together every morning, and especially at night....Have a little family altar where both husband and wife, and children, gather to offer deep devotion unto God and unite their souls forever in ever-joyous Cosmic Consciousness .... * The more you meditate together, the deeper your love for one another will grow.

Friendship

Friendship is God's trumpet call, bidding the soul

* See glossary.

destroy the partitions of ego-consciousness that separate it from all other souls and from Him.

❖ ❖ ❖

Friendship is the purest form of God's love because
it is born of the heart's free choice and is not imposed
upon us by familial instinct. Ideal friends never part;
nothing can sever their fraternal relationship.

❖ ❖ ❖

The treasure of friendship is your richest possession, because it goes with you beyond this life. All
the true friends you have made you will meet again
in the home of the Father, for real love is never lost.

❖ ❖ ❖

When perfect friendship exists either between
two hearts or within a group of hearts in a spiritual
relationship, such friendship perfects each individual.

❖ ❖ ❖

There is a magnet in your heart that will attract
true friends. That magnet is unselfishness, thinking
of others first. Very few persons are free from self-
centeredness. Yet one can develop the quality of unselfishness very easily if he practices thinking of others first.

❖ ❖ ❖

You cannot attract true friends without removing
from your own character the stains of selfishness and
other unlovely qualities. The greatest art of making
friends is to behave divinely yourself—to be spiritual,

to be pure, to be unselfish....The more your human shortcomings drop away and divine qualities come into your life, the more friends you will have.

❖ ❖ ❖

True friendship consists in being mutually useful in offering one's friend good cheer in distress, sympathy in sorrow, advice in trouble, and material help in times of real need....One who has given his friendship to another gladly foregoes selfish pleasures or self-interest for the sake of his friend's happiness, without consciousness of loss or sacrifice, and without counting the cost.

❖ ❖ ❖

No matter what difference of opinion there is between you and such friends, there is always understanding and communication. In that relationship, regardless of differing views, you have mutual respect and cherish your friendship above everything else. True friendship established in God is the only relationship that is lasting.

❖ ❖ ❖

If you proffer friendship, you must mean it. You must not show kindness or cooperation outside, and inside feel the opposite. Spiritual law is very powerful. Don't go against spiritual principles. Never deceive or be treacherous. As a friend, know when to mind your own business; understand your place; know when you should have the willingness to cooperate, and when you should have the will to noncooperate.

❖ ❖ ❖

It is wrong to speak the truth when, by doing so, one betrays another person unnecessarily and to no good purpose. Suppose a man drinks, but tries to hide it from the rest of the world. You know about his weakness, and so in the name of truthfulness you announce to your friends, "You know that so and so drinks, don't you?" Such a remark is uncalled for; one should not be busy about other people's business. Be protective about others' personal faults, so long as they harm no one else. Speak privately to an offender about his failings, if you have an opportunity or responsibility to help him; but never, under pretext of helping someone, speak deliberately to hurt him. You will only "help" him to become your enemy. You may also extinguish any desire that he might have had to become better.

❖ ❖ ❖

Help your friend by being a mental, aesthetic, and spiritual inspiration to him. Never be sarcastic to a friend. Do not flatter him unless it is to encourage him. Do not agree with him when he is wrong.

❖ ❖ ❖

Be true, be sincere, and friendship will steadily grow. I remember a discussion with Sri Yukteswar about sincerity. I had said, "Sincerity is everything."

"No," he responded, "sincerity plus thoughtfulness is everything." He went on: "Suppose you are sitting in the parlor in your home, and there is a beautiful new carpet on the floor. It is raining outside. A friend you haven't seen in many years flings open the door and rushes into the room to greet you."

"That is all right," I said. But my Guru had yet to make his point.

"You were sincerely happy to see each other," he said, "but wouldn't you have liked it better if he had been thoughtful enough to take off his muddy boots before he came in and ruined the carpet?"

I had to agree he was right.

No matter how well you think of someone, or how close you are to that person, it is important to sweeten that relationship with good manners and thoughtfulness. Then friendship becomes truly wonderful and enduring. Familiarity that leads you to be inconsiderate is very harmful to friendship.

❖ ❖ ❖

Just as dew helps the flower to grow, so inner and outer sweetness fosters the growth of friendship.

❖ ❖ ❖

Friendship is noble, fruitful, holy —
When two separate souls march in difference
Yet in harmony; agreeing and disagreeing,
Glowingly improving diversely....
Ah, friendship—flowering, heaven-born plant!
Nurtured art thou in the soil of measureless love,
In the seeking of soul progress together
By two who would smooth the way, each for
      the other.*

* From the poem "Friendship," in *Songs of the Soul* by Paramahansa Yogananda.

❖ ❖ ❖

To be a true, unconditional friend, your love must be anchored in God's love. Your life with God is the inspiration behind true divine friendship with all.

❖ ❖ ❖

Try to perfect your friendship with a few souls. When you can truly give unconditional friendship to them, then your heart will be ready to give perfect friendship to all. And when you can do that, you become divine—like God and the great ones, who give friendship to every being, irrespective of personality. Friendship that remains centered on only one or two souls, to the exclusion of others, is like a river that loses itself in the sands, never reaching the ocean. The river of divine friendship broadens as it flows onward, powerful and truthful, eventually merging in the oceanic presence of God.

Affirmation

As I radiate love and goodwill to others, I will open the channel for God's love to come to me. Divine love is the magnet that draws to me all good.

CHAPTER 12

Understanding Death

Though the ordinary man looks upon death with dread and sadness, those who have gone before know it as a wondrous experience of peace and freedom.

❖ ❖ ❖

Perhaps we wonder most of all about those we love. Where are they? Why are they spirited away from us? A brief goodbye, and then they disappear behind the veil of death. We feel so helpless and sad; and there is nothing we can do about it....When someone is dying, though he cannot speak, a desire is expressed in his consciousness. He is thinking, "I am leaving my loved ones; will I ever see them again?" And those whom he is leaving behind also think, "I am losing him. Will he remember me? Will we meet again?"... When I lost my mother in this life, I promised myself that I would never again be attached to anyone.* I gave my love to God. That first experience with death was very serious for me. But through it I learned much. I searched undaunted for months and years until I found the answer to the mystery of life and death....What I tell you, I have experienced.

* Paramahansa Yogananda was only eleven years old when his mother died. He stormed the very gates of heaven with his youthful spiritual determination until he experienced response from God and the realization that it is God's love expressing through the forms of all our loved ones. To love God is to love all without exclusiveness or the inevitable pain associated with attachment. *(Publisher's Note)*

❖ ❖ ❖

At death, you forget all the limitations of the physical body and realize how free you are. For the first few seconds there is a sense of fear—fear of the unknown, of something unfamiliar to the consciousness. But after that comes a great realization: the soul feels a joyous sense of relief and freedom. You know that you exist apart from the mortal body.

❖ ❖ ❖

Every one of us is going to die someday, so there is no use in being afraid of death. You don't feel miserable at the prospect of losing consciousness of your body in sleep; you accept sleep as a state of freedom to look forward to. So is death; it is a state of rest, a pension from this life. There is nothing to fear. When death comes, laugh at it. Death is only an experience through which you are meant to learn a great lesson: you cannot die.

❖ ❖ ❖

Our real self, the soul, is immortal. We may sleep for a little while in that change called death, but we can never be destroyed. We exist, and that existence is eternal. The wave comes to the shore, and then goes back to the sea; it is not lost. It becomes one with the ocean, or returns again in the form of another wave.* This body has come, and it will vanish; but the soul essence within it will never cease to exist. Nothing can terminate that eternal consciousness.

* A reference to reincarnation. See glossary.

❖ ❖ ❖

Even a particle of matter or a wave of energy is indestructible, as science has proved; the soul or spiritual essence of man is also indestructible. Matter undergoes change; the soul undergoes changing experiences. Radical changes are termed death, but death or a change in form does not change or destroy the spiritual essence.

❖ ❖ ❖

The body is only a garment. How many times you have changed your clothing in this life, yet because of this you would not say that *you* have changed. Similarly, when you give up this bodily dress at death you do not change. You are just the same, an immortal soul, a child of God.

❖ ❖ ❖

The word "death" is a great misnomer, for there is no death; when you are tired of life, you simply take off the overcoat of flesh and go back to the astral world.*

❖ ❖ ❖

The Bhagavad Gita† speaks beautifully and solacingly of the immortality of the soul:

> Never the spirit was born; the spirit shall cease to be never;
> Never was time it was not; End and Beginning are dreams!
> Birthless and deathless and changeless remaineth the

* Heaven, the subtle region of higher forces and consciousness. See *astral world* in glossary.
† II:20, Sir Edwin Arnold's translation.

spirit forever;
Death hath not touched it at all, dead though the
    house of it seems.

❖ ❖ ❖

Death is not the end: it is temporary emancipa-
tion, given to you when karma, the law of justice, determines that your present body and environment
have served their purpose, or when you are too weary
or exhausted by suffering to bear the burden of physical existence any longer. To those who are suffering,
death is resurrection from the painful tortures of flesh
into awakened peace and calmness. To the elderly, it
is a pension earned by years of struggling through life.
For all, it is a welcome rest.

❖ ❖ ❖

When you reflect that this world is filled with
death, and that your body, too, has to be relinquished,
God's plan seems very cruel. You can't imagine that
He is merciful. But when you look at the process of
death with the eye of wisdom, you see that after all
it is merely a thought of God passing through a nightmare of change into blissful freedom in Him again.
Saint and sinner alike are given freedom at death, to
a greater or lesser degree according to merit. In the
Lord's dream astral world—the land to which souls
go at death—they enjoy a freedom such as they never
knew during their earthly life. So don't pity the person who is passing through the delusion of death, for
in a little while he will be free. Once he gets out of
that delusion, he sees that death was not so bad after

all. He realizes his mortality was only a dream and rejoices that now no fire can burn him, no water can drown him; he is free and safe.*

❖ ❖ ❖

The consciousness of the dying man finds itself suddenly relieved of the weight of the body, of the necessity to breathe, and of any physical pain. A sense of soaring through a tunnel of very peaceful, hazy, dim light is experienced by the soul. Then the soul drifts into a state of oblivious sleep, a million times deeper and more enjoyable than the deepest sleep experienced in the physical body....The after-death state is variously experienced by different people in accordance with their modes of living while on earth. Just as different people vary in the duration and depth of their sleep, so do they vary in their experiences after death. The good man who works hard in the factory of life goes into a deep, unconscious, restful sleep for a short while. He then awakens in some region of life in the astral world: "In my Father's house are many mansions."†

❖ ❖ ❖

"I have never been able to believe in heaven," a new student remarked. "Is there truly such a place?"

---

* "No weapon can pierce the soul; no fire can burn it; no water can moisten it; nor can any wind wither it . . . . The soul is immutable, all-permeating, ever calm, and immovable—eternally the same. The soul is said to be imponderable, unmanifested, and unchangeable. Therefore, knowing it to be such, thou shouldst not lament" (Bhagavad Gita II:23–25).
† John 14:2.

"Yes," Paramahansa Yogananda replied. "Those who love God and put their trust in Him go there when they die. On that astral plane, one has power to materialize anything immediately by sheer thought. The astral body is made of shimmering light. In those realms colors and sounds exist that earth knows nothing about. It is a beautiful and enjoyable world."

❖ ❖ ❖

[Death] is not the end of things, but a transfer from physical experiences in the gross domain of changeable matter to purer joys in the astral realm of multicolored lights.

❖ ❖ ❖

"The astral world is infinitely beautiful, clean, pure, and orderly," [Sri Yukteswar said]. "There are no dead planets or barren lands. The terrestrial blemishes — weeds, bacteria, insects, snakes — are absent. Unlike the variable climates and seasons of the earth, the astral planets maintain the even temperature of an eternal spring, with occasional luminous white snow and rain of many-colored lights. Astral planets abound in opal lakes and bright seas and rainbow rivers."

❖ ❖ ❖

Souls in the astral region are clothed in gossamer light. They do not encase themselves in bundles of bones with fleshly covers. They carry no frail, heavy frames that collide with other crude solids and break. Therefore, there is no war in the astral land between man's body and solids, oceans, lightning, and disease.

Nor are there accidents, for all things coexist in mutual helpfulness, rather than antagonism. All forms of vibration function in harmony with one another. All forces live in peace and conscious helpfulness. The souls, the rays on which they tread, and the orange rays they drink and eat, all are made of living light. Souls live in mutual cognizance and cooperation, breathing not oxygen, but the joy of Spirit.

❖ ❖ ❖

"Friends of other lives easily recognize one another in the astral world," [Sri Yukteswar said]. "Rejoicing at the immortality of friendship, they realize the indestructibility of love, often doubted at the time of the sad, delusive partings of earthly life."

❖ ❖ ❖

Why do we cry when our dear ones die? Because we sorrow for our own loss. If our loved ones leave us for training in better schools of life, we should rejoice instead of being selfishly sad, for we may keep them earthbound and hamper their progress by broadcasting our own selfish wills. The Lord is ever new, and by His infinite magic wand, Renewing Death, He keeps each created object, each living being, ever manifesting, ever remodeling itself into a fitter vehicle for His inexhaustible expressions. Death comes to dutiful men as a promotion to a higher state; it comes to failures to give them another chance in a different environment.

❖ ❖ ❖

Death is the culmination of life. In death life seeks rest. It is precursor to the greatest happiness, the exquisite freedom from all tortures of flesh. Death automatically dismisses all bodily pain, just as sleep banishes the weariness and aches of the hard-worked body. Death is a parole from the prison of the physical body.

❖ ❖ ❖

How glorious is life after death! No more will you have to lug about this old baggage of bones, with all its troubles. You will be free in the astral heaven, unhindered by physical limitations.

❖ ❖ ❖

I once wrote about a vision I had of a dying youth, in which God showed me the right attitude toward death. The youth was lying in bed and was told by his doctors that he had just one day to live. He replied, "One day to reach my Beloved! when death shall open the gates of immortality and I shall be free from the prison bars of pain. Don't cry for me, ye who are left on this desolate shore, still to mourn and deplore; it is I who pity you. You weep for me dark tears, crying for your loss in me; but I weep for you joyous tears, because I am going before you, for your welfare's sake, to light candles of wisdom all the way. And I shall wait to welcome you there where I shall be, with my only Beloved and yours. O dear ones, rejoice in my joy!"*

* Paramahansa Yogananda here paraphrases his poem, "The Dying Youth's Divine Reply," from *Songs of the Soul.*

❖ ❖ ❖

You don't know what is going to come to you in this world; you have to go on living and worrying. Those who die are pitying us; they are blessing us. Why should you grieve for them? I told this [story of the dying youth] to a woman who had lost her son. When I finished explaining, she dried her tears immediately and said, "Never before have I felt such peace. I am glad to know that my son is free. I thought something awful had happened to him."

❖ ❖ ❖

When a dear one dies, instead of grieving unreasonably, realize that he has gone on to a higher plane at the will of God, and that God knows what is best for him. Rejoice that he is free. Pray that your love and goodwill be messengers of encouragement to him on his forward path. This attitude is much more helpful. Of course, we would not be human if we did not miss loved ones; but in feeling lonesome for them we don't want selfish attachment to be the cause of keeping them earthbound. Extreme sorrow prevents a departed soul from going ahead toward greater peace and freedom.

❖ ❖ ❖

[There is a right kind of sorrow in the face of death, as expressed by Paramahansa Yogananda in the memorial service he conducted for Sri Gyanamata, one of his earliest and foremost disciples, whom he lovingly and respectfully referred to as "Sister."*]

* See page 35.

Someone said to me last night, when there were tears in my eyes, that I should be happy that Sister is free in the joy of Spirit. I said, "I know all that, how happy Sister is, how this glorious chapter of her life is closed, how the pain is gone from her body....My spirit is with hers in God. But these are tears of love, that on this side I shall miss her...."

That bright and humble light that was Sister was extinguished before me, and has commingled with the Great Light. That is my contentment, and my sadness. And I am glad to be sad, glad that she was with us to inspire so much love from our hearts.

❖ ❖ ❖

To send your thoughts to loved ones who have passed on, sit quietly in your room and meditate upon God. When you feel His peace within you, concentrate deeply at the Christ center,* the center of will at the point between the two eyebrows, and broadcast your love to those dear ones who are gone. Visualize at the Christ center the person you wish to contact. Send to that soul your vibrations of love, and of strength and courage. If you do this continuously, and if you don't lose the intensity of your interest in that loved one, that soul will definitely receive your vibrations. Such thoughts give your loved ones a sense of well-being, a sense of being loved. They have not forgotten you any more than you have forgotten them.

❖ ❖ ❖

* See glossary.

Send your thoughts of love and goodwill to your loved ones as often as you feel inclined to do so, but at least once a year—perhaps on some special anniversary. Mentally tell them, "We will meet again sometime and continue to develop our divine love and friendship with one another." If you send them your loving thoughts continuously now, someday you will surely meet them again. You will know that this life is not the end, but merely one link in the eternal chain of your relationship with your loved ones.

Affirmation

The ocean of Spirit has become the little bubble of my soul. Whether floating in birth, or disappearing in death, in the ocean of cosmic awareness the bubble of my life cannot die. I am indestructible consciousness, protected in the bosom of Spirit's immortality.

CHAPTER 13

The Consummate Goal

Mankind is engaged in an eternal quest for that "something else" he hopes will bring him happiness, complete and unending. For those individual souls who have sought and found God, the search is over: He is that Something Else.

❖ ❖ ❖

Many people may doubt that finding God is the purpose of life; but everyone can accept the idea that the purpose of life is to find happiness. I say that God is Happiness. He is Bliss. He is Love. He is Joy that will never go away from your soul. So why shouldn't you try to acquire that Happiness? No one else can give it to you. You must continuously cultivate it yourself.

❖ ❖ ❖

Even if life gave you at one time everything you wanted — wealth, power, friends — after a while you would again become dissatisfied and need something more. But there is one thing that can never become stale to you — joy itself. Happiness that is delightfully varied, though its essence is changeless, is the inner experience everyone is seeking. Lasting, ever-new joy is God. Finding this Joy within, you will find it in everything without. In God you will tap the Reservoir of perennial, unending bliss.

❖ ❖ ❖

Suppose you are going to be punished by not being allowed to go to sleep when you are desperately in need of rest, and suddenly someone says: "All right, you may go to sleep now." Think of the joy you would feel just before falling asleep. Multiply that one million times! Still it would not describe the joy felt in communion with God.

❖ ❖ ❖

The joy of God is boundless, unceasing, all the time new. Body, mind, nothing can disturb you when you are in that consciousness—such is the grace and glory of the Lord. And He will explain to you whatever you haven't been able to understand; everything you want to know.

❖ ❖ ❖

When you sit in the silence of deep meditation, joy bubbles up from within, roused by no outer stimulus. The joy of meditation is overwhelming. Those who have not gone into the silence of true meditation do not know what real joy is.

❖ ❖ ❖

As the mind and the feeling are directed inward, you begin to feel God's joy. The pleasures of the senses do not last; but the joy of God is everlasting. It is incomparable!

Making Time for God in Your Life

Everything has its place, but when you waste time at the cost of your true happiness it is not good.

I dropped every unnecessary activity so that I could meditate and try to know God, so that I could day and night be in His divine consciousness.

❖ ❖ ❖

Very few of us know how much we can put into life if we use it properly, wisely, and economically. Let us economize our time — lifetimes ebb away before we wake up, and that is why we do not realize the value of the immortal time God has given us.

❖ ❖ ❖

Do not while away your time in idleness. A great many people occupy themselves with inconsequential activities. Ask them what they have been doing and they will usually say, "Oh, I have been busy every minute!" But they can scarcely remember what they were so busy about!

❖ ❖ ❖

In an instant you may be required to leave this world; you will have to cancel all your engagements. Why then give any other activity first importance, with the result that you have no time for God? That is not common sense. It is because of *maya*, the net of cosmic delusion which is thrown over us, that we entangle ourselves in mundane interests and forget the Lord.

❖ ❖ ❖

Belief in the necessity of fulfilling lesser desires and duties first is man's greatest delusion. I well remember that during my training as a young disciple of my guru, Swami Sri Yukteswarji, I kept promising myself daily, "I will meditate longer tomorrow." A whole year slipped by before I realized that I was still putting it off. At once I made a resolution that first thing in the morning I would clean my body and then meditate long. But even then, as soon as I stirred about I became caught up in my daily duties and activities. Thereupon I resolved to have my meditation first. Thus I learned a great lesson: First comes my duty to God, and then I take care of all lesser duties.

❖ ❖ ❖

It is important to differentiate between your needs and your wants. Your needs are few, while your wants can be limitless. In order to find freedom and Bliss, minister only to your needs. Stop creating limitless wants and pursuing the will-o'-the-wisp of false happiness.

❖ ❖ ❖

"What is the best prayer?" a disciple inquired. Paramahansa Yogananda replied:

"Say to the Lord: 'Please tell me Thy will.' Don't say: 'I want this and I want that,' but have faith that He knows what you need. You will see that you get much better things when He chooses for you."

❖ ❖ ❖

If you have no success in receiving some little toy of matter with which you are infatuated, be not resentful toward God. Sometimes it is good that we do not get the things we want. When the Divine Father sees that His impulsive children want to plunge into the flames of wrong or excessive desires, lured by their luminosity, He tries to protect them from being burned.

God says: "When My children think they do not receive from Me any response to their prayers, they know not that I do answer — only differently from what they expect of Me. I will not always respond according to their wishes, until they have attained perfection. Only when they are perfect will their requests be governed always by wisdom."

❖ ❖ ❖

It is not wrong to tell the Lord that we want something, but it shows greater faith if we simply say: "Heavenly Father, I know that Thou dost anticipate my every need. Sustain me according to Thy will."

If a man is eager to own a car, for instance, and prays for it with sufficient intensity, he will receive it. But possession of a car may not be the best thing for him. Sometimes the Lord denies our little prayers because He intends to bestow on us a better gift. Trust more in God. Believe that He who created you will maintain you.

❖ ❖ ❖

God has proven that when He is with me all the "necessities of life" become unnecessary. In that consciousness you become more healthy than the average person, more joyous, more bountiful in every way. Don't seek little things; they will divert you from God. Start your experiment now: make life simple and be a king.

❖ ❖ ❖

The ordinary person is influenced by his worldly environment. The man of concentration shapes his own life. He plans his day and finds at the end of the day that his plans are carried out; he finds himself nearer to God and his goal. A weak man plans many wonderful things, but finds at the end of the day that he has been a victim of circumstances and bad habits. Such a person usually blames everyone but himself.

Remember, you should blame no one but yourself for your troubles. If you make up your mind that you are going to control your circumstances according to law, your circumstances will adjust themselves accordingly. Eventually you must learn to lead a controlled existence.

❖ ❖ ❖

You are the master of the moments of your life.

❖ ❖ ❖

Suppose you tell yourself, "Now today I will find time to meditate." *Do* it; sit for at least a few minutes. The next day, resolve to stay a little longer in meditation. And the next day, in spite of obstacles, make a little more effort.

❖ ❖ ❖

Not until you feel in your consciousness the absolute importance of God will you reach Him. Do not permit life to cheat you. Form those good habits that make for true happiness. Follow a simple diet, exercise the body, and meditate daily — no matter what happens, rain or shine. If you are unable to exercise and meditate in the morning, do it at night. Pray to Him every day, "Lord, even if I die, or if the whole world crumbles away, I am going to find time daily to be with Thee."

❖ ❖ ❖

The minutes are more important than the years. If you do not fill the minutes of your life with thoughts of God, the years will slip by; and when you need Him most you may be unable to feel His presence. But if you fill the minutes of your life with divine aspirations, automatically the years will be saturated with them.

Practicing the Presence of God

Joy lies in continually thinking of God. The longing for Him should be constant. A time comes when your mind never wanders away, when not even the greatest affliction of body, mind, and soul can take your consciousness from the living presence of God. Is that not wonderful? to live and think and feel God all the time? to remain in the castle of His presence, whence death nor aught else can take you away?

❖ ❖ ❖

Just behind the words of your speech, just behind your thoughts, just behind the love of your heart, just behind your will, just behind your sense of I-ness, is the great spirit of God. For those who think Him far away, He is far away; but for those who think Him near, He is ever near. The Bhagavad Gita says, "He who perceives Me everywhere, and beholds everything in Me, never loses sight of Me, nor do I ever lose sight of him."* The Lord never fails us.

❖ ❖ ❖

We say that God is invisible to us, but in reality He is visible in the mighty manifested universe. God is everything—not just one thing.

❖ ❖ ❖

As you look upon creation, which appears so solid and real, remember always to think of it as the thought of God, frozen into physical forms. You can condition your mind to this realization in little ways each day. Whenever you see a beautiful sunset, think to yourself: "It is God's painting on the sky." As you look into the face of each person you meet, think within: "It is God who has become that form." Apply this trend of thought to all experiences: "The blood in my body is God; the reason in my mind is God; the love in my heart is God; everything that exists is God."

❖ ❖ ❖

Yoga is the art of doing everything with the consciousness of God. Not only when you are meditating, but also when you are working, your thoughts should be constantly anchored in Him. If you work with the consciousness that you are doing it to please God, that activity unites you with Him. Therefore do not imagine that you can find God only in meditation. Both meditation and right activity are essential, as the Bhagavad Gita teaches. If you think of God

* Bhagavad Gita VI:20.

while you perform your duties in this world, you will
be mentally united with Him.

❖ ❖ ❖

When you work for God, not self, it is just as good
as meditation. Then work helps your meditation and
meditation helps your work. You need the balance.
With meditation only, you become lazy. With activity
only, the mind becomes worldly and you forget God.

❖ ❖ ❖

Doing things for God is a very personal experience, so satisfying.

❖ ❖ ❖

It is when you persistently, selflessly perform
every action with love-inspired thoughts of God that
He will come to you. Then you realize that you are
the Ocean of Life, which has become the tiny wave
of each life. This is the way of knowing the Lord
through activity. When in every action you think of
Him before you act, while you are performing the action, and after you have finished it, He will reveal
Himself to you. You must work, but let God work
through you; this is the best part of devotion. If you
are constantly thinking that He is walking through
your feet, working through your hands, accomplishing through your will, you will know Him.

❖ ❖ ❖

No matter what you may be doing you are always
free to whisper your love to God, until you con-

sciously receive His response. This is the surest way to contact Him in the mad rush of present-day life.

❖ ❖ ❖

Of greatest help in your development is the habit of mental whispering to God. You will see a change in yourself that you will like very much. No matter what you do, God should be constantly in your mind. When you want to see a special show, or to buy a dress or a car you have admired, is it not true that no matter what else you may be doing your mind is continually thinking how you can get those things? Until you fulfill your strong desires, your mind will not rest; it ceaselessly works toward fulfilling those desires. Your mind should be on God night and day in the same way. Transmute petty desires into one great desire for Him. Your mind should continually whisper, "Night and day, night and day, I look for Thee night and day."*

❖ ❖ ❖

That is the philosophy of life by which we should live. Not tomorrow, but today, this minute. There cannot be any excuse for not thinking of God. Day and night, rolling in the background of your mind, God! God! God! instead of money or sex or fame. Whether you are washing dishes or digging a ditch or working in an office or a garden — whatever you may be doing — inwardly say, "Lord, manifest to me! You are right here.

* From "Door of My Heart," published in *Cosmic Chants* by Paramahansa Yogananda.

You are in the sun. You are in the grass. You are in the water. You are in this room. You are in my heart."

❖ ❖ ❖

Every thought we think sets up a particular subtle vibration.... When you mentally utter the word "God," and keep on repeating that thought within, it sets up a vibration that invokes the presence of God.

❖ ❖ ❖

Whenever your mind wanders in the maze of myriad worldly thoughts, patiently lead it back to remembrance of the indwelling Lord. In time you will find Him ever with you—a God who talks with you in your own language, a God whose face peeps at you from every flower and shrub and blade of grass. Then you shall say: "I am free! I am clothed in the gossamer of Spirit; I fly from earth to heaven on wings of light." And what joy will consume your being!

Establishing a Relationship With God

"It hardly seems practical to think about God all the time," a visitor remarked. Paramahansaji replied:

"The world agrees with you, and is the world a happy place? True joy eludes the man who forsakes God, because He is Bliss Itself. On earth His devotees live in an inner heaven of peace; but those who forget Him pass their days in a self-created hades of insecurity and disappointment. To 'make friends' with the Lord is to be really practical!"

❖ ❖ ❖

Cultivate His acquaintance. It is possible to know God just as well as you know your dearest friend. That is the truth.

❖ ❖ ❖

First you must have a right concept of God — a definite idea through which you can form a relationship with Him — and then you must meditate and pray until that mental conception becomes changed into actual perception. Then you will know Him. If you persist, the Lord will come.

❖ ❖ ❖

There are people who depict their Creator as one who imperiously tests man with the smoke of ignorance and the fire of punishment, and who judges man's actions with heartless scrutiny. They thus distort the true concept of God as a loving, compassionate Heavenly Father into a false image of one who is a strict, unsparing, and vengeful tyrant. But devotees who commune with God know it is foolish to think of Him otherwise than as the Compassionate Being who is the infinite receptacle of all love and goodness.

❖ ❖ ❖

God is Eternal Bliss. His being is love, wisdom, and joy. He is both impersonal and personal, and manifests Himself in whatever way He pleases. He appears before His saints in the form each of them holds dear: a Christian sees Christ, a Hindu beholds Krishna or the Divine Mother, and so on. Devotees whose worship takes an impersonal turn become conscious of the Lord as an infinite Light or as the wondrous sound of *Aum*, the primal Word, the Holy Ghost. The highest experience man can have is to feel that Bliss in which every other aspect of Divinity—love, wisdom, immortality—is fully contained.

But how can I convey to you in words the nature of God? He is ineffable, indescribable. Only in deep meditation shall you know His unique essence.

Proof of God's Response

"Sir, I do not seem to be progressing in my meditations. I see and hear nothing," a student said. Paramahansa Yogananda replied:

"Seek God for His own sake. The highest perception is to feel Him as Bliss, welling up from your infinite depths. Don't yearn for visions, spiritual phenomena, or thrilling experiences. The path to the Divine is not a circus!"

❖ ❖ ❖

A common cause of spiritual discouragement is the devotee's expectation that God's response will come in a great blaze of awe-inspiring inner illumination. This erroneous notion dulls the devotee's perception of the subtle Divine responses that are present from the very beginning of one's meditative practices. God responds to the devotee's every effort, every devotional call. Even as a novice, you will realize this in your own seeking if you learn to recognize Him as the quiet, inner peace that steals over your consciousness. This peace is the first proof of God's presence within. You will know it is He who has guided and inspired you to some right decision in your life. You will feel His strength empowering you to overcome bad habits and nurture spiritual qualities. You will know Him as the ever-increasing joy and love that surges deep within, overflowing into your everyday life and relationships.

❖ ❖ ❖

The more you feel peace in meditation, the closer you are to God. He moves nearer and nearer to you the deeper you enter into meditation. The peace of meditation is the language and embracing comfort of God. Therefore, God is present right on the throne of peace within you. Find Him there first and you will find Him in all the noble pursuits of life, in true friends, in the beauty of nature, in good books, in good thoughts, in noble aspirations . . . . When you know God as peace within, then you will realize Him as peace existing in the universal harmony of all things without.

❖ ❖ ❖

"Though I try to calm my mind, I lack the power to banish restless thoughts and to penetrate the world within," a visitor remarked. "I must be lacking in devotion."

"Sitting in the silence trying to feel devotion may often get you nowhere," Paramahansa Yogananda said. "That is why I teach scientific techniques of meditation. Practice them and you will be able to disconnect the mind from sensory distractions and from the otherwise ceaseless flow of thoughts.

"By *Kriya Yoga* one's consciousness functions on a higher plane; devotion to the Infinite Spirit then arises spontaneously in man's heart."

❖ ❖ ❖

The essential proof of Self-realization—of God's consciousness in you — is to be truly and unconditionally happy. If you are receiving more and more joy in meditation, without cessation, you may know that God is making manifest His presence in you.

❖ ❖ ❖

Even true devotees think sometimes that God does not answer their prayers. He does answer silently, through His laws; but until He is absolutely sure of the devotee He will not answer openly, He will not talk to the devotee. The Lord of Universes is so humble that He does not speak, lest in so doing He influence the devotee's use of free will to choose or reject Him. Once you know Him, there is no doubt that you will love Him. Who could resist the Irresistible? But you have to prove your unconditional love for God in order to know Him. You have to have faith. You have to know that even as you pray He is listening to you. Then He will make Himself known to you.

❖ ❖ ❖

When God does not respond to your prayers, it is because you are not in earnest. If you offer Him dry imitation prayers, you cannot expect to claim the

Heavenly Father's attention. The only way to reach God through prayer is by persistence, regularity, and depth of earnestness. Cleanse your mind of all negation, such as fear, worry, anger; then fill it with thoughts of love, service, and joyous expectation. In the sanctum of your heart there must be enshrined one power, one joy, one peace—God.

The Personal Element in the Search for God

There is a personal element in the search for God that is more important than mastery over the whole science of Yoga. The Heavenly Father wants to be sure that His children desire only Him, that they will not be satisfied with anything else. When God is made to feel that He is not first in the devotee's heart, He stands aside. But to him who says, "O Lord, it matters not if I lose sleep tonight, so long as I am with Thee," He will come. Positively! From behind the countless screens of this mysterious world the Ruler of creation will come forth to reveal Himself behind each one. He talks to His true devotees, and plays hide-and-seek with them. Sometimes He suddenly unveils a comforting truth when one is worried. In time, and in direct or indirect ways, He grants every wish of His devotee.

❖ ❖ ❖

To coax God to give Himself takes steady, unceasing zeal. Nobody can teach you that zeal. You have to develop that yourself. "You can take a horse to water but you cannot make him drink." Yet when the horse is thirsty it seeks out water with zeal. So,

when you have an immense thirst for the Divine,
when you will not give undue importance to anything else—the tests of the world or the tests of the
body—then He will come.

❖ ❖ ❖

The greatest factor for success with God is to
have that resolute desire.

❖ ❖ ❖

Though God hears all our prayers He doesn't always respond. Our situation is like that of a child
who calls for his mother, but the mother doesn't
think it necessary to come. She sends him a plaything
to keep him quiet. But when the child refuses to be
comforted by anything except the mother's presence,
she comes. If you want to know God, you must be
like the naughty baby who cries till the mother comes.

❖ ❖ ❖

Do not jump up after only one or two mental
broadcasts, but with continuous personal zeal keep
on consciously [affirming] with the ever increasing
hunger of your heart, incessantly...until you feel the
ever increasing thrill of joy bursting in your whole
body.

❖ ❖ ❖

When you feel a bursting thrill of joy expanding
in your heart and your whole body, and it continues
to increase even after meditation, you have received
the one sure proof that God has answered through the
devotion-tuned radio of your heart.

❖ ❖ ❖

In Him you will find all the love of all hearts. You will find completeness. Everything that the world gives you and then takes away, leaving you in pain or disillusionment, you will find in God in a much greater way, and with no aftermath of sorrow.

❖ ❖ ❖

He is the nearest of the near, the dearest of the dear. Love Him as a miser loves money, as an ardent man loves his sweetheart, as a drowning person loves breath. When you yearn for God with intensity, He will come to you.

❖ ❖ ❖

The Searcher of Hearts wants only your sincere love. He is like a little child: someone may offer Him his whole wealth and He doesn't want it; and another cries to Him, "O Lord, I love you!" and into that devotee's heart He comes running.

❖ ❖ ❖

God will not tell you that you should desire Him above all else, because He wants your love to be freely given, without "prompting." That is the whole secret in the game of this universe. He who created us yearns for our love. He wants us to give it spontaneously, without His asking. Our love is the one thing God does not possess, unless we choose to bestow it. So, you see, even the Lord has something to attain: our love. And we shall never be happy until we give it.

❖ ❖ ❖

The greatest love you can experience is in communion with God in meditation. The love between the soul and Spirit is the perfect love, the love you are all seeking. When you meditate, love grows. Millions of thrills pass through your heart . . . . If you meditate deeply, a love will come over you such as no human tongue can describe; you will know His divine love, and you will be able to give that pure love to others.

❖ ❖ ❖

If you could feel even a particle of divine love, so great would be your joy — so overpowering — you could not contain it.

❖ ❖ ❖

If we are attuned to God, our perception is limitless, pervading everywhere in the oceanic flow of the Divine Presence. When the Spirit is known, and when we know ourselves as Spirit, there is no land or sea, no earth or sky — all is He. The melting of everything in Spirit is a state no one can describe. A great bliss is felt — eternal fullness of joy and knowledge and love.

❖ ❖ ❖

The love of God, the love of the Spirit, is an all-consuming love. Once you have experienced it, it shall lead you on and on in the eternal realms. That love will never be taken away from your heart. It shall burn there, and in its fire you shall find the great magnetism of Spirit that draws others unto you, and attracts whatsoever you truly need or desire.

I tell you truthfully that all my questions have been answered, not through man but through God. He *is.* He *is.* It is His spirit that talks to you through me. It is His love that I speak of. Thrill after thrill! Like gentle zephyrs His love comes over the soul. Day and night, week after week, year after year, it goes on increasing — you don't know where the end is. And that is what you are seeking, every one of you. You think you want human love and prosperity, but behind these it is your Father who is calling you. If you realize He is greater than all His gifts, you will find Him.

❖ ❖ ❖

Man has come on earth solely to learn to know God; he is here for no other reason. This is the true message of the Lord. To all those who seek and love Him, He tells of that great Life where there is no pain, no old age, no war, no death—only eternal assurance. In that Life nothing is destroyed. There is only ineffable happiness that will never grow stale — a happiness always new.

So that is why it is worthwhile to seek God. All those who sincerely seek Him will surely find Him. Those who want to love the Lord and yearn to enter His kingdom, and who sincerely wish in their hearts to know Him, will find Him. You must have an ever-increasing desire for Him, day and night. He will acknowledge your love by fulfilling His promise to you throughout eternity, and you shall know joy and happiness unending. All is light, all is joy, all is peace, all is love. He is all.

❖ ❖ ❖

Prayers and Affirmations

*Teach me to find Thy presence on the altar of
my constant peace and in the joy that springs
from deep meditation.*

❖ ❖ ❖

*Bless me, that I may find Thee in the temple
of each thought and activity. Finding Thee
within, I will find Thee without, in all people,
and in all conditions.*

About the Author

*"The ideal of love for God and service to humanity
found full expression in the life of Paramahansa
Yogananda....Though the major part of his life was
spent outside India, still he takes his place among
our great saints. His work continues to grow and
shine ever more brightly, drawing people everywhere on the path of the pilgrimage of the Spirit."*

In these words, the Government of India paid trib-
ute to the founder of Self-Realization Fellowship/Yogoda
Satsanga Society of India,* upon issuing a commemora-
tive stamp in his honor on March 7, 1977, the twenty-
fifth anniversary of his passing.

Paramahansa Yogananda began his life's work in India in 1917 with the founding of a "how-to-live" school
for boys, where modern educational methods were combined with yoga training and instruction in spiritual
ideals. In 1920 he was invited to Boston as India's representative to an International Congress of Religious
Liberals. Subsequent lectures in Boston, New York, and
Philadelphia were enthusiastically received, and in 1924
he embarked on a cross-continental speaking tour.

For the next decade Paramahansaji traveled exten-
sively, giving lectures and classes in which he instructed
thousands in the yoga science of meditation and balanced spiritual living. In 1925 he established the Self-
Realization Fellowship International Headquarters in
Los Angeles, and from there the spiritual and human-
itarian work he began continues today under the guidance of one of his foremost disciples, Sri Daya Mata,
president of Self-Realization Fellowship. In addition to
publishing Paramahansa Yogananda's writings, lectures,
and informal talks (including a comprehensive series of

* See glossary.

lessons on the science of Kriya Yoga meditation), the society oversees Self-Realization temples, retreats, and meditation centers around the world; monastic training programs; and a Worldwide Prayer Circle, which serves as a channel to help bring healing to those in need and greater peace and harmony among all nations.

Quincy Howe, Jr., Ph.D., Professor of Ancient Languages, Scripps College, wrote: "Paramahansa Yogananda brought to the West not only India's perennial promise of God-realization, but also a practical method by which spiritual aspirants from all walks of life may progress rapidly toward that goal .... Originally appreciated in the West only on the most lofty and abstract level, the spiritual legacy of India is now accessible as practice and experience to all who aspire to know God, not in the beyond, but in the here and now....Yogananda has placed within the reach of all the most exalted methods of contemplation."

The life and teachings of Paramahansa Yogananda are described in his *Autobiography of a Yogi*, which has remained a classic in its field since its publication in 1946 and is now used as a text and reference work in many colleges and universities.

Autobiography of a Yogi

"A rare account."—*New York Times*

"A fascinating and clearly annotated study."—*Newsweek*

"There has been nothing before, written in English or any other European language, like this presentation of Yoga." — *Columbia University Press*

"These pages reveal, with incomparable strength and clarity, a fascinating life, a personality of such unheard-of greatness, that from beginning to end the reader is left breathless. We must credit this book with the power to bring about a spiritual revolution." — *Schleswig-Holsteinische Tagespost*, Germany

PARAMAHANSA YOGANANDA:
A Yogi in Life and Death

Paramahansa Yogananda entered *mahasamadhi* (a yogi's final conscious exit from the body) in Los Angeles, California, on March 7, 1952, after concluding his speech at a banquet held in honor of H. E. Binay R. Sen, Ambassador of India.

The great world teacher demonstrated the value of yoga (scientific techniques for God-realization) not only in life but in death. Weeks after his departure his unchanged face shone with the divine luster of incorruptibility.

Mr. Harry T. Rowe, Los Angeles Mortuary Director, Forest Lawn Memorial-Park (in which the body of the great master is temporarily placed), sent Self-Realization Fellowship a notarized letter from which the following extracts are taken:

"The absence of any visual signs of decay in the dead body of Paramahansa Yogananda offers the most extraordinary case in our experience....No physical disintegration was visible in his body even twenty days after death....No indication of mold was visible on his skin, and no visible desiccation (drying up) took place in the bodily tissues. This state of perfect preservation of a body is, so far as we know from mortuary annals, an unparalleled one....At the time of receiving Yogananda's body, the Mortuary personnel expected to observe, through the glass lid of the casket, the usual progressive signs of bodily decay. Our astonishment increased as day followed day without bringing any visible change in the body under observation. Yogananda's body was apparently in a phenomenal state of immutability....

"No odor of decay emanated from his body at any time. . . . The physical appearance of Yogananda on March 27th, just before the bronze cover of the casket was put into position, was the same as it had been on March 7th. He looked on March 27th as fresh and as unravaged by decay as he had looked on the night of his death. On March 27th there was no reason to say that his body had suffered any visible physical disintegration at all. For these reasons we state again that the case of Paramahansa Yogananda is unique in our experience."

AIMS AND IDEALS
of
Self-Realization Fellowship
As set forth by Paramahansa Yogananda, Founder
Sri Daya Mata, President

To disseminate among the nations a knowledge of definite scientific techniques for attaining direct personal experience of God.

To teach that the purpose of life is the evolution, through self-effort, of man's limited mortal consciousness into God Consciousness; and to this end to establish Self-Realization Fellowship temples for God-communion throughout the world, and to encourage the establishment of individual temples of God in the homes and in the hearts of men.

To reveal the complete harmony and basic oneness of original Christianity as taught by Jesus Christ and original Yoga as taught by Bhagavan Krishna; and to show that these principles of truth are the common scientific foundation of all true religions.

To point out the one divine highway to which all paths of true religious beliefs eventually lead; the highway of daily, scientific, devotional meditation on God.

To liberate man from his threefold suffering: physical disease, mental inharmonies, and spiritual ignorance.

To encourage "plain living and high thinking"; and to spread a spirit of brotherhood among all peoples by teaching the eternal basis of their unity: kinship with God.

To demonstrate the superiority of mind over body, of soul over mind.

To overcome evil by good, sorrow by joy, cruelty by kindness, ignorance by wisdom.

To unite science and religion through realization of the unity of their underlying principles.

To advocate cultural and spiritual understanding between East and West, and the exchange of their finest distinctive features.

To serve mankind as one's larger Self.

Glossary

astral world. Behind the physical world of matter, there exists a subtle astral world of light and energy, and a causal or ideational world of thought. Every being, every object, every vibration on the physical plane has an astral counterpart, for in the astral universe (heaven) is the "blueprint" of the material universe. At death each individual, though freed from his physical encasement, remains clothed in an astral body of light (similar in appearance to the earthly form left behind) and a causal body of thought. He ascends to one of the many vibratory regions of the astral world ("In my Father's house are many mansions." — John 14:2) to continue his spiritual evolution in the greater freedom of that subtle realm. There he remains for a karmically predetermined time until physical rebirth. (See *reincarnation.*)

Aum (Om). The Sanskrit root word or seed-sound symbolizing that aspect of Godhead which creates and sustains all things; Cosmic Vibration. *Aum* of the Vedas became the sacred word *Hum* of the Tibetans; *Amin* of the Moslems; and *Amen* of the Egyptians, Greeks, Romans, Jews, and Christians. The world's great religions state that all created things originate in the cosmic vibratory energy of *Aum* or Amen, the Word or Holy Ghost. "In the beginning was the Word, and the Word was with God, and the Word was God .... All things were made by him [the Word or *Aum*]; and without him was not any thing made that was made" (John 1:1,3).

Amen in Hebrew means *sure, faithful.* "These

things saith the Amen, the faithful and true witness, the beginning of the creation of God" (Revelation 3:14). Even as sound is produced by the vibration of a running motor, so the omnipresent sound of *Aum* faithfully testifies to the running of the "Cosmic Motor," which upholds all life and every particle of creation through vibratory energy. In the *Self-Realization Fellowship Lessons (q.v.)*, Paramahansa Yogananda teaches techniques of meditation whose practice brings direct experience of God as *Aum* or Holy Ghost. That blissful communion with the invisible divine Power ("the Comforter, which is the Holy Ghost" — John 14:26) is the truly scientific basis of prayer.

avatar. Divine incarnation; from the Sanskrit *avatara*, with roots *ava*, "down," and *tri*, "to pass." One who attains union with Spirit and then returns to earth to help mankind is called an avatar.

Bhagavad Gita. "Song of the Lord." An ancient Indian scripture consisting of eighteen chapters from the *Mahabharata* epic. Presented in the form of a dialogue between the avatar *(q.v.)* Lord Krishna and his disciple Arjuna on the eve of the historic battle of Kurukshetra, about 3000 B.C., the Gita is a profound treatise on the science of Yoga (union with God) and a timeless prescription for happiness and success in everyday living. Of this universal scripture Mahatma Gandhi wrote: "Those who will meditate on the Gita will derive fresh joy and new meanings from it every day. There is not a single spiritual tangle which the Gita cannot unravel."

The quotations from the Bhagavad Gita in the text and footnotes of this book are from translations by Paramahansa Yogananda, which he rendered from the Sanskrit sometimes literally and sometimes in paraphrase.

Bhagavan Krishna. An avatar *(q.v.)* who lived in India

three millenniums before the Christian era. One of the meanings given for the word *Krishna* in the Hindu scriptures is "Omniscient Spirit." Thus, *Krishna*, like *Christ*, is a title signifying the spiritual magnitude of the avatar — his oneness with God. (See *Christ Consciousness.*) The title *Bhagavan* means "Lord."

Christ center. The center of concentration and will in the body, at the point between the eyebrows. Seat of Christ Consciousness *(q.v.)* and of the spiritual eye *(q.v.)*.

Christ Consciousness. "Christ" or "Christ Consciousness" is the projected consciousness of God immanent in all creation. In Christian scripture it is called the "only begotten son," the only pure reflection in creation of God the Father; in Hindu scripture it is called *Kutastha Chaitanya*, the cosmic intelligence of Spirit everywhere present in creation. It is the universal consciousness, oneness with God, manifested by Jesus, Krishna, and other avatars. Great saints and yogis know it as the state of *samadhi (q.v.)* meditation wherein their consciousness has become identified with the intelligence in every particle of creation; they feel the entire universe as their own body.

Cosmic Consciousness. The Absolute; Spirit beyond creation. Also the *samadhi*-meditation state of oneness with God both beyond and within vibratory creation.

Divine Mother. The aspect of God that is active in creation; the *shakti*, or power, of the Transcendent Creator. Other terms for this aspect of Divinity are Nature or *Prakriti*, *Aum*, Holy Ghost, Cosmic Intelligent Vibration. Also, the personal aspect of God as Mother, embodying the Lord's love and compassionate qualities.

The Hindu scriptures teach that God is both immanent and transcendent, personal and impersonal. He may be sought as the Absolute; as one of His manifest eternal qualities, such as love, wisdom, bliss, light; or in a concept such as Heavenly Father, Mother, Friend.

egoism. The ego-principle, *ahamkara* in Sanskrit (lit., "I do"), is the root cause of dualism or the seeming separation between man and his Creator. Egoism brings human beings under the sway of *maya (q.v.)*, by which the soul becomes delusively identified with the limitations of body-consciousness and forgets its oneness with God, the Sole Doer. (See *Self.*)

guru. Spiritual teacher. Though the word *guru* is often misused to refer simply to any teacher or instructor, a true God-illumined guru is one who, in his attainment of self-mastery, has realized his identity with the omnipresent Spirit. Such a one is uniquely qualified to lead the seeker on his or her inward journey toward divine realization.

karma. Effects of past actions, from this or previous lifetimes; from the Sanskrit *kri,* to do. The equilibrating law of karma is that of action and reaction, cause and effect, sowing and reaping. In the course of natural righteousness, every human being by his thoughts and actions becomes the molder of his own destiny. Whatever energies he himself, wisely or unwisely, has set in motion must return to him as their starting point, like a circle inexorably completing itself. An understanding of karma as the law of justice serves to free the human mind from resentment against God and man. A person's karma follows him from incarnation to incarnation until fulfilled or spiritually transcended. (See *reincarnation.*)

Krishna. See *Bhagavan Krishna.*

Kriya Yoga. A sacred spiritual science, originating millenniums ago in India. It includes certain techniques of meditation *(q.v.)* whose devoted practice leads to direct, personal experience of God. *Kriya,* a form of *Raja* ("royal" or "complete") *Yoga*, is extolled by Krishna in the Bhagavad Gita and by Patanjali in the *Yoga Sutras. Kriya Yoga* was revived in this age by Mahavatar Babaji *(q.v.)*, who chose Paramahansa Yogananda to make this holy science available worldwide and to establish a society to insure that it would be preserved in pure form for future generations. *Kriya Yoga* is explained in chapter 26 of *Autobiography of a Yogi*, and is taught to students of the *Self-Realization Fellowship Lessons* who fulfill certain spiritual requirements.

Lahiri Mahasaya. *Lahiri* was the family name of Shyama Charan Lahiri (1828–1895). *Mahasaya*, a Sanskrit religious title, means "large-minded." Lahiri Mahasaya was a disciple of Mahavatar Babaji, and the guru of Swami Sri Yukteswar (Paramahansa Yogananda's guru). Lahiri Mahasaya was the one to whom Babaji revealed the ancient, almost lost science of *Kriya Yoga (q.v.)*. A seminal figure in the renaissance of Yoga in modern India, he gave instruction and blessing to countless seekers who came to him, without regard to caste or creed. He was a Christlike teacher with miraculous powers; but also a family man with business responsibilities, who demonstrated for the modern world how an ideally balanced life can be achieved by combining meditation with right performance of outer duties. Lahiri Mahasaya's life is described in *Autobiography of a Yogi*.

Mahavatar Babaji. The deathless *mahavatar* ("great *avatar*") who in 1861 taught *Kriya Yoga (q.v.)* to Lahiri Mahasaya, and thereby restored to the world the spiritual science that had been lost for centuries. More information about his life and spiritual mission is given in *Autobiography of a Yogi*. (See *avatar*.)

maya. The delusory power inherent in the structure of creation, by which the One appears as many. *Maya* is the principle of relativity, inversion, contrast, duality, oppositional states; the "Satan" (lit., in Hebrew, "the adversary") of the Old Testament prophets; and the "devil" whom Christ described picturesquely as a "murderer" and a "liar," because "there is no truth in him" (John 8:44).

Paramahansa Yogananda wrote:

"The Sanskrit word *maya* means 'the measurer'; it is the magical power in creation by which limitations and divisions are apparently present in the Immeasurable and Inseparable. *Maya* is Nature herself—the phenomenal worlds, ever in transitional flux as antithesis to Divine Immutability.

"In God's plan and play *(lila)*, the sole function of Satan or *maya* is to attempt to divert man from Spirit to matter, from Reality to unreality. 'The devil sinneth from the beginning. For this purpose the Son of God was manifested, that he might destroy the works of the devil' (I John 3:8). That is, the manifestation of Christ Consciousness, within man's own being, effortlessly destroys the illusions or 'works of the devil.'

"*Maya* is the veil of transitoriness in Nature, the ceaseless becoming of creation; the veil that each man must lift in order to see behind it the Creator, the changeless Immutable, eternal Reality."

"Man is able to create both matter and consciousness in an illusory dream world; therefore it should not be difficult for him to realize that Spirit, utilizing the power of *maya*, has created for man a dream world of 'life' or conscious existence that in essence is as false (because ephemeral, ever changing) as are man's experiences in the dream state....Man in his mortal aspect dreams of dualities and contrasts — life and death, health and disease, happiness and sorrow; but when he awakens in soul consciousness all dualities disappear and he knows himself as the eternal and blissful Spirit."

meditation. Concentration upon God. The term is used in a general sense to denote practice of any technique for interiorizing the attention and focusing it on some aspect of God. In the specific sense, meditation refers to the end result of successful practice of such techniques: direct experience of God through intuitive perception. It is the seventh step *(dhyana)* of the eightfold path of Yoga described by Patanjali, achieved only after one has attained that fixed concentration within whereby he is completely undisturbed by sensory impressions from the outer world. In deepest meditation one experiences the eighth step of the Yoga path: *samadhi (q.v.)*, communion, oneness with God. (See also *Yoga.)*

paramahansa. A spiritual title signifying one who has attained the highest state of unbroken communion with God. It may be conferred only by a true guru on a qualified disciple. Swami Sri Yukteswar bestowed the title on his beloved disciple Yogananda in 1935. *Paramahansa* literally means "supreme swan." In the Hindu scriptures, the *hansa* or swan symbolizes spiritual discrimination.

prana. Life energy or life force. Intelligent, finer-than-atomic energy; life-principle of the physical cosmos and basic substance of the astral world *(q.v.)*. In the physical world, there are two kinds of *prana:* (1) the cosmic vibratory energy that is omnipresent in the universe, structuring and sustaining all things; (2) the specific *prana* or energy that pervades and sustains each human body.

reincarnation. The doctrine that human beings, compelled by the law of evolution, incarnate repeatedly in progressively higher lives—retarded by wrong actions and desires, and advanced by spiritual endeavors — until Self-realization and God-union are attained. Having thus transcended the limitations and imperfections of mortal consciousness, the soul is forever freed from compulsory reincarnation. "Him that overcometh will I make a pillar in the temple of my God, and he shall go no more out" (Revelation 3:12).

The concept of reincarnation is not exclusive to eastern philosophy, but was held as a fundamental truth of life by many ancient civilizations. The early Christian Church accepted the principle of reincarnation, which was expounded by the Gnostics and by numerous Church fathers, including Clement of Alexandria, Origen, and St. Jerome. It was not until the Second Council of Constantinople in A.D. 553 that the doctrine was officially removed from church teachings. Today many Western thinkers are beginning to adopt the concept of the law of karma *(q.v.)* and reincarnation, seeing in it a grand and reassuring explanation of life's seeming inequities.

samadhi. Ecstasy; superconscious experience; ultimately, union with God as the all-pervading supreme Reality. (See *superconsciousness* and *Yoga*.)

Self. Capitalized to denote the *atman* or soul, the divine essence of man, as distinguished from the ordinary self, which is the human personality or ego. The Self is individualized Spirit, whose essential nature is ever-existing, ever-conscious, ever-new joy. The Self or soul is man's inner fountainhead of love, wisdom, peace, courage, compassion, and all other divine qualities.

Self-realization. Paramahansa Yogananda has defined Self-realization as follows: "Self-realization is the knowing — in body, mind, and soul — that we are one with the omnipresence of God; that we do not have to pray that it come to us, that we are not merely near it at all times, but that God's omnipresence is our omnipresence; that we are just as much a part of Him now as we ever will be. All we have to do is improve our knowing."

Self-Realization Fellowship. The society founded by Paramahansa Yogananda in the United States in 1920 (and as Yogoda Satsanga Society of India in 1917) for disseminating worldwide the spiritual principles and meditation techniques of *Kriya Yoga (q.v.)*. (See "About the Author," page 179.) Paramahansa Yogananda has explained that the name Self-Realization Fellowship signifies "fellowship with God through Self-realization, and friendship with all truth-seeking souls." (See also "Aims and Ideals of Self-Realization Fellowship," page 182.)

Self-Realization Fellowship Lessons. The teachings of Paramahansa Yogananda, compiled into a comprehensive series of lessons for home study and made available to sincere truth seekers all over the world. These lessons contain the yoga meditation techniques taught by Paramahansa Yogananda, including, for those who fulfill certain requirements, *Kriya Yoga (q.v.)*. Information about the *Lessons* is available on request from Self-Realization Fellowship International Headquarters.

spiritual eye. The single eye of intuition and omnipresent perception at the Christ *(Kuthastha)* center *(q.v.)* (*ajna chakra*) between the eyebrows; the entryway into the ultimate states of divine consciousness. Jesus referred to the divine light that is perceived through the spiritual eye when he said: "When thine eye is single, thy whole body also is full of light....Take heed therefore that the light which is in thee be not darkness" (Luke 11:34–35).

Sri Yukteswar, Swami. (1855–1936). A Christlike master of modern India; guru of Paramahansa Yogananda; and author of *The Holy Science,* a treatise on the underlying unity of Christian and Hindu scriptures. Sri Yukteswarji's life is described in Paramahansa Yogananda's *Autobiography of a Yogi.*

superconsciousness. The pure, intuitive, all-seeing, ever-blissful consciousness of the soul. Sometimes used generally to refer to all the various states of God-communion experienced in meditation, but specifically the initial state, wherein one transcends ego-consciousness and realizes his Self as soul, made in the image of God. Thence follow the higher states of realization: Christ-consciousness and cosmic consciousness *(q.v.)*.

Yoga. From Sanskrit *yuj,* "union." Yoga means union of the individual soul with Spirit; also, the methods by which this goal is attained. There are various types of yoga methods; the one taught by Self-Realization Fellowship is *Raja Yoga,* the "royal" or "complete" yoga taught by Bhagavan Krishna in the Bhagavad Gita. The sage Patanjali, foremost ancient exponent of Yoga, has outlined eight definite steps by which the *Raja Yogi* attains *samadhi,* or union with God. These are (1) *yama,* moral conduct; (2) *niyama,* religious observances; (3) *asana,* right posture to still bodily restlessness; (4) *pranayama,* control of *prana,* subtle life currents; (5) *pratyahara,* interiorization; (6) *dharana,* concentration; (7) *dhyana,* meditation; and (8) *samadhi,* superconscious experience.

yogi. One who practices Yoga *(q.v.).* He or she may be either married or unmarried, either a person of worldly responsibilities or one who has taken formal religious vows.

Yogoda Satsanga Society of India. The name by which Paramahansa Yogananda's society is known in India. The Society was founded by him in 1917. Its headquarters, Yogoda Math, is situated on the banks of the Ganges at Dakshineswar, near Calcutta, with a branch *math* at Ranchi, Bihar. In addition to meditation centers and groups throughout India, Yogoda Satsanga Society has twenty-one educational institutions, from primary through college level. The literal meaning of

Yogoda, a word coined by Paramahansa Yogananda, is "that which yoga imparts," i.e., Self-realization. *Satsanga* means "divine fellowship," or "fellowship with Truth." For the West, Paramahansaji translated the Indian name as "Self-Realization Fellowship" *(q.v.)*.

Index